What people are saying about …

HELL IS REAL (BUT I HATE TO ADMIT IT)

"Hell is one of those Bible truths that most of us would rather keep out of sight—sort of like the crazy uncle who shows up and wrecks an otherwise-perfect family gathering. In *Hell Is Real (But I Hate to Admit It),* Brian Jones shines the light on both the theology and the practical implications of this all-too-neglected topic—and he does it all in a highly readable and accessible way. That's no easy task. This is one of those books I'll keep on my library shelf for a long time. I think you'll do the same."

Larry Osborne, pastor of North Coast Church
and author of *Sticky Church*

"There is an abundance of good books, but not many that are important. This is one of the few. It's a book you *need* to read."

Vince Antonucci, author of *I Became a Christian and All I Got Was This Lousy T-shirt* and *Guerrilla Lovers*

"The modern-day church is guilty of talking an inordinate amount about the grace of God and a miniscule amount about the wrath of God. Brian Jones tackles a tough topic and does so both biblically and graciously. The world doesn't need to be told it's going to hell. It needs to be shown how to get to heaven. Brian Jones does just that!"

Dave Stone, senior minister of
Southeast Christian Church

"In a time when many are trying to do away with hell, Jones accepts its reality without compromise and shows us biblically why we must do the same. In addition, this book comes straight from Jones's heart. In it we are confronted with sound doctrine but are also moved by the author's personal testimonies and by the abundance of illustrative ministry experiences that appear throughout. Jones not only effectively convicts us of the 'apocalyptic urgency' of warning sinners about hell but also gives very down-to-earth lessons on how to evangelize. I hope every Christian reads this book and every preacher uses it as a sermon resource."

Jack W. Cottrell, professor of theology
at Cincinnati Christian University

"At a time when some pastors are denying the reality of hell, Brian Jones's engaging work provides a welcome antidote to this heresy. Great stories and fresh illustrations are woven together with sound biblical teaching to produce a book that is a readable, often humorous account of why there is a hell. I especially appreciate that this is a practical book, full of real-life application we can all use to lead others to an eternity in heaven as opposed to hell."

Bob Russell, retired senior minister
of Southeast Christian Church

"Brian Jones is a courageous voice of truth, grace, and love. His writing always challenges me, and his life inspires me. This book moves me, as it will you. It will be a significant tool for our dialogue on an important subject. The stakes couldn't be higher."

Gene Appel, senior pastor of
Eastside Christian Church

"With a pastor's heart and a strong biblical grasp, Brian Jones shows the importance of having an eternal perspective for today. *Hell Is Real (But I Hate to Admit It)* will challenge you to reconsider the Bible's teaching on this important topic and to work out the practical implication for our lives. Compassionately written and intelligently argued, this is a message we should all wrestle with and take to heart."

Jud Wilhite, author of *Throw It Down* and senior
pastor of Central Christian Church, Las Vegas

HELL IS REAL (BUT I HATE TO ADMIT IT)

HELL IS REAL (BUT I HATE TO ADMIT IT)

BRIAN JONES

HELL IS REAL (BUT I HATE TO ADMIT IT)
Published by David C Cook
4050 Lee Vance View
Colorado Springs, CO 80918 U.S.A.

David C Cook Distribution Canada
55 Woodslee Avenue, Paris, Ontario, Canada N3L 3E5

David C Cook U.K., Kingsway Communications
Eastbourne, East Sussex BN23 6NT, England

David C Cook and the graphic circle C logo
are registered trademarks of Cook Communications Ministries.

The author has added italics to Scripture and quotations for emphasis.

LCCN 2011927399
ISBN 978-0-7814-0572-0
eISBN 978-1-4347-0417-7

Published in association with literary agent Jenni Burke
of D.C. Jacobson & Associates LLC, an Author Management Company
www.dcjacobson.com
Portions of chapter one were also previously published by Standard
Publishing in *Second Guessing God: Hanging on When You Can't See
His Plan* in 2006 © Brian Jones, ISBN 978-0-7847-1841-4

The Team: Alex Field, Amy Konyndyk, Nick Lee, Renada Arens, and Karen Athen
Cover Design: JWH Graphic Arts, James Hall

Printed in the United States of America
First Edition 2011

2 3 4 5 6 7 8 9 10

081011

DEDICATION

For a lifetime of quietly "living with reverence" and "teaching what is good" (Titus 2:3), I dedicate this to my mother, Darlene Jones. On the final day, many will be in heaven, looking to you, with gratitude.

CONTENTS

PART ONE

IF HELL IS REAL ... WHY DON'T I BELIEVE IT?

1

ETERNAL DAMNATION, REALLY?

> The great Christian revolutions come not by the discovery of something that was not known before. They happen when somebody takes radically something that was always there.
>
> —*H. Richard Niebuhr*[1]

My three daughters know that I have one sacred, unbreakable rule when our family drives anywhere on vacation: If you have to go to the bathroom once we're on the highway, you better have a Pringles can close by because we're not stopping.

I've learned the hard way that when it comes to small bladders, you have to exert martial law on the whole van. Otherwise you'll spend half your vacation touring the country's finest rest stops and eating twelve times the daily recommended allowance of pork rinds. In fact, after years of driving to remote vacation spots, I've learned four key principles for a successful road trip with kids: Keep 'em sleeping, keep 'em separated, keep 'em dehydrated, and keep 'em watching videos. If complaining erupts, I've also found it helpful to have memorized Bill Cosby's classic line: "I brought you into this world; I can take you out!"[2]

There have been times, however, I've been tempted to break my own rules. For instance, I'll never forget the time we drove from Dayton, Ohio, to Dallas. We had just stopped in Louisville to fill up, and after twenty minutes we had successfully emptied all the bladders, gotten situated with our snacks, and pulled back on the road heading toward the highway. Suddenly, out of the corner of my eye, I saw a plume of smoke rising from the rooftop of a small apartment complex. I looked for a chimney but saw none. I reassured myself that surely someone had already called 911 and everything would be fine.

Besides, I thought, *I can't even tell for sure if there's a fire.*

Yet something inside of me kept wondering, *What if I'm the only person who is seeing this right now?* As I approached the onramp I went back and forth in my head, *Should we stop? Should we keep going? Should we stop? We don't have time for this! But what if I'm the only person*—I swerved to the left at the last second, drove past the onramp, and circled back into the apartment complex. My guilt (or basic human decency) had won out.

As I pulled up I discovered that it was in fact a fire, and by then the flames had engulfed a large part of the roof. Worse, my suspicion was accurate—we were the only ones there. I asked my wife, Lisa, to call 911, and then I ran inside to warn people to get out.

Once I reached the third floor, I frantically started to bang on the doors, one by one, but at each door there was no response. I then ran down to the second floor and did the same. As I was about to go down to the first floor, a shirtless young man with disheveled hair stuck his head out of one of the second-floor units. He cracked the door open, and as I ran back to meet him, I was hit with a wall of marijuana smoke.

"Yo, my man, what's up?" he said with a slight grin.

"What's up is that your apartment is about to burn to the ground. Put your joint down and help me get people out of here!"

We ran down the steps to the first floor. Two couples responded to our knocking. "There's an elderly lady on the third floor!" one woman shouted. "Did you get her out?"

My heart sank. After racing back up to the third floor, we began furiously pounding on her door. The first-floor neighbor yelled, "She gets confused easily. We may have to break down the door." But just as she said that the handle slowly began to turn. Coughing, confused, and minutes away from being consumed by the fire, she followed her neighbors down to safety. As we stepped out the front door, we heard sirens in the distance. After we guided the elderly woman into the hands of the paramedics, I turned around and watched the firemen storm up the apartment steps to stop the blaze.

As I stood there, the weight of it all hit me. I let out a deep sigh and thought to myself, *What would have happened if I had kept driving?*

A few hours later, when my adrenaline had finally worn down and the kids were asleep, a bizarre thought came out of nowhere. I call it a "thought" because to this day I'm still not sure if what popped into my mind came from God or from the triple stack of chocolate chip pancakes from IHOP digesting in my stomach. Here's what came to my mind:

> *Let me get this straight: You're willing to run into a burning building to save someone's life, but non-Christians all around you are going to hell and you don't believe it, let alone lift a finger to help.*

Admittedly, I was a little freaked out by the "thought," but at the time I blew it off as a lingering remnant of my conservative-evangelical upbringing.

Four years prior to this event I had graduated from seminary, and with the endless boxes of books I lugged into the moving truck when I left, I also packed my watered-down theology, a healthy dose of skepticism about biblical authority, and a nail-tight conviction that hell was a mythological concept that no loving and thinking Christian could accept. I had weighed the evidence, read all the books, and sat at the feet of experts for three years. Now the verdict was in—the Bible's teaching about hell was inaccurate at best and hateful at worst. What I was taught as a child was a lie, and now that I was becoming a pastor, I was sure I'd never perpetuate that ridiculous myth again.

OBJECTIONS TO HELL

Undoubtedly, you're a smart person. You like to read, and you were intrigued enough by the topic of hell and eternal damnation to give this book a go (either that or the bookstore didn't have that Dan Brown novel you were looking for). And so I think you can understand the six good reasons it seemed ridiculous to me that God would send anyone to hell. Read through these objections and see if you resonate with how I felt.

1. Hell Is a Very Unpopular Idea

Hell has always been an unpopular concept, and for obvious reasons. According to a recent survey by The Pew Forum on Religion and Public Life, only 59 percent of Americans believe in hell.[3] That's six out of ten people, a slight majority in any room. But another poll narrowed the question even more and discovered that "fewer than half of all Americans (43 percent) thought people go to heaven or hell depending on their actions on earth."[4] Furthermore, in twenty-five years of being a pastor, I would add that *maybe* three out of every ten Christians I've met truly believe people who die without becoming Christians go to hell.

The fact that so few people believe in hell made me wonder if it was about as factual as the lost city of Atlantis.

2. The Punishment Doesn't Fit the Crime

To my postseminary self, sending someone to hell for all eternity seemed tantamount to sending someone to death row for stealing a postage stamp. Enduring physical, emotional, and spiritual torture not just for a year, or ten years, or billions of years on end, *but for all eternity*—it just didn't seem fair. In fact, it seemed hateful and absurd. Who would propose such a punishment on anyone for anything done in this life? Atheist William C. Easttom put it this way,

> God says, "Do what you wish, but make the wrong choice and you will be tortured for eternity in hell." That … would be akin to a man telling his girlfriend, do what you wish, but if you choose to leave me, I will track you down and blow your brains out. When a man says this we call him a psychopath and cry out for his imprisonment/execution. When God says the same we call him "loving" and build churches in his honor.[5]

When I looked at it from this vantage point, I understood why Tertullian, a well-known pastor in the early church, wrote, "We get ourselves laughed at for proclaiming that God will one day judge the world."[6] In eighteen hundred years that sentiment hasn't really changed.

3. Life Is Hell Enough

The more I thought about the concept of eternal punishment, the more I kept thinking to myself, *Don't most people go through enough hell in one lifetime?* Think about all the suffering people go through in this life. Hell just didn't make any sense to me. One blogger does a fantastic job of illustrating this point:

> Given life's headaches, backaches, toothaches, strains, scrapes, cuts, rashes, burns, bruises, breaks, PMS, fatigue, hunger, odors, molds, colds, parasites, viruses, cancers, genetic defects, blindness, deafness, paralysis, retardation, deformities, ugliness, embarrassments, miscommunications, confused signals, ignorance, unrequited love, dashed hopes, boredom, hard labor, repetitious labor, old age, accidents, fires, floods, earthquakes, typhoons, tornadoes, hurricanes, and volcanoes, I cannot see how anyone, after they're dead, deserves "eternal punishment" too.[7]

4. Hell Seems Intolerant and Hateful

One of the biggest things that weighed on me was how cruel and arrogant the concept of hell sounded when I talked about it with good friends of mine who weren't Christians.

A friend once asked me, "How can you believe my great-grandparents who brutally suffered and died in the Holocaust won't go to heaven just because they didn't believe in Jesus? They were loving, God-fearing people." I didn't have a good answer, and the lack of an answer that sounded loving and moral troubled me immensely. The vast majority of people on this planet think that believing anyone—except people like Hitler who commit heinous crimes against humanity—would go to hell is arrogant, insensitive, ignorant, and hateful.

Victor Hugo wrote, "Hell is an outrage on humanity. When you tell me that your deity made you in his image, I reply that he must have been very ugly."[8] I had to agree. *What kind of God would send anyone to hell?* I thought.

5. Respected Evangelical Scholars Reject the Idea of Hell

What troubled me even more was that everywhere I turned, noted Christian scholars confirmed my inner struggle. For instance, evangelical theologian Clark Pinnock wrote,

> I consider the concept of hell as endless torment in body and mind an outrageous doctrine.... How can Christians possibly project a deity of such cruelty and vindictiveness whose ways include inflicting everlasting torture upon his creatures, however sinful they may have been? Surely a God who would do such a thing is more nearly like Satan than like God.[9]

Statements like this made sense to me. Knowing that highly educated people like Pinnock and others thought this way gave me more confidence that it might be okay to veer away from my traditional Christian beliefs if I chose to do so. If they veered from clear biblical teachings, why couldn't I?

6. I Like Being Liked

Finally, truth be told, the need to be liked was a real factor in my personal struggle. I hated the fact that I could have friendships with people, but if I stayed true to my Christian beliefs, I felt like I had to spend all my time and energy trying to convert them. I wanted to embrace them, cherish their uniqueness, understand their beliefs, and celebrate our diverse cultural and religious upbringings. Hell was an affront to all of this. I didn't want to be thought of as the nutty, intolerant guy who was always trying to get people to admit that they were sinners in need of a Savior. I wanted to be the cool, relevant, and intelligent pastor people liked and wanted their friends to know.

Do you resonate with any of those objections to hell?

AN UNEXPECTED CONFRONTATION

The combined weight of the attacks by my professors and the sheer immorality of the idea itself finally broke the theological dam open for me. Over time I simply gave up on the idea, *proudly*. The problem was that believing the Bible is God's Word is, well, up near the top of any pastor's job description, at least in an evangelical church. I needed a job, so I came up with what seemed like a simple solution: I would never tell anyone about my disbelief. In fact, I carried my secret around for four years after graduate school without ever telling anyone, not the people who went to my church, not the staff with whom I worked, not my friends, not even my wife. The secret was so well hidden that sometimes I was able to forget about it—until that apartment fire in Louisville, and then again a few months later at a monastery in northwest Ohio.

I was in the habit of going to a monastery roughly once a month for a spiritual retreat. I would arrive early in the day to pray, journal, take long walks in the woods, and leave late in the afternoon. On one such retreat I felt an overwhelming sense of spiritual pressure, the spiritual equivalent of the kind of pressure you feel in your ears when swimming in deep water. I sensed that something was wrong, but I didn't know what it was. For the better part of the day, I locked myself into a cold, cement-block room and asked God to show me the source of my consternation.

For the first three hours, I heard nothing—my prayers seemed as if they were bouncing off the ceiling. By noon I felt like I was starting to make a connection with God, but I wasn't prepared for what happened next, when I felt God's Spirit impress upon my heart, "Brian, this charade has to end. You're a pastor and your job is to teach people the Bible, but you don't believe what you're teaching. You don't believe in hell."

I was a little startled, so I picked up my Bible and did something I had up to that point discouraged people in my church from doing—I played what I call "Bible Roulette." In his book *Formula for a Burning Heart,* A. W. Tozer said, "An honest man with an open Bible and a pad and pencil is sure to find out what is wrong with him very quickly."[10] I can attest to the truth of that statement.

I closed my eyes, wildly fanned the pages back and forth, and randomly pointed to passages and read them. The first passage was about eternal punishment. I looked up at the ceiling and said, "That's a coincidence." The second passage was about God's wrath. This time I felt a little uneasy. Then I did it a third time and couldn't believe my eyes—*eternal punishment again*. I'm not usually the most mystical person in the world, but I slowly closed the pages of my Bible, put it down on the table next to me, and said, "I get the message." Church leaders must "keep hold of the deep truths of the faith with a clear conscience" (1 Tim. 3:9), and hell is one of those "deep truths."

I spent the next five hours reading and underlining every passage about hell in the New Testament, and as I did, I felt an overwhelming sense of conviction. What I discovered shocked me. I had always assumed that the Bible contained only a few scattered references to hell. I was wrong; hell is taught everywhere.

Take the book of Matthew, for instance, just one book among twenty-seven in the entire New Testament. Here is what we learn about hell from that book alone:

Twelve separate passages record Jesus' teachings about the judgment of nonbelievers and their assignment to eternal punishment.[11] Matthew 13:49–50 summarizes them all: "This is how it will be at the end of the age. The angels will come and separate the wicked from the righteous and throw them into the blazing furnace, where there will be weeping and gnashing of teeth."

Jesus employed the most graphic language to describe what hell is like: *fire* (Matt. 5:22; 18:9); *eternal fire* (18:8); *destruction* (7:13); *away from his presence* (7:23); *thrown outside* (8:12; 22:13; 25:30); *blazing furnace* (13:42); *darkness* (22:13; 25:30); *eternal punishment* (25:46); *weeping and gnashing of teeth* (8:12; 13:42; 13:50; 22:13; 24:51).

Jesus twice used the word *eternal* (18:8; 25:46) to convey that the punishment of nonbelievers would continue forever.

As I moved from the Gospels into the rest of the New Testament, I was struck by how the writers unashamedly addressed the issue. There is no hesitancy or apology in their words. The basic tone is, "This is a reality. Now let's get out there and tell people how to avoid it." Second Thessalonians 1:7–9 summarizes what these other New Testament authors taught:

> This will happen when the Lord Jesus is revealed from heaven in blazing fire with his powerful angels. He will punish those who do not know God and do not obey the gospel of our Lord Jesus. They will be punished with everlasting destruction and shut out from the presence of the Lord and from the glory of his might.

My heart raced as I flipped page after page after page. I discovered, by the end of my study, that the New Testament's teaching about hell is not an ambiguous topic supported by a few hard-to-understand passages. It is inescapable: Virtually every book in the New Testament underscores some aspect of the reality of hell. Jesus taught it; Paul, Peter, and every early church leader taught it, but I wasn't teaching it. I realized I had a decision to make. Could I discount what Jesus taught about hell if I based my belief in heaven on similar passages in the same books?

Could it be possible that Jesus' disciples actually had some of the same reservations I had but still persisted in teaching it because they knew in the depths of their souls that hell was real? Wasn't my hesitancy to believe in hell a sign of my compassion for people? Yet, if hell really exists, and I knew that but wasn't willing to tell people how to avoid it, wouldn't that also be the most extreme form of cruelty imaginable? Most of all, could it be that I was ultimately basing my acceptance of this teaching more on what people thought of me than on whether I felt it was intellectually plausible?

As the weight of it all finally set in, I dropped to my knees, stretched out my arms and legs to the sides, and fell prostrate on the unfinished concrete monastery floor. Not content, however, with the act of simply lying facedown, I shoved my face over and over against the concrete as if an invisible hand pushed against the base of my neck. I buried my face in the silence and wept. After an hour or so passed, I just couldn't stomach listening to myself any longer. I stood up, gathered my belongings, and walked out of the monastery retreat house I had rented for the day. While my planning retreat certainly didn't end quite like I thought it would, I left knowing exactly what I needed to do.

I drove straight home and met Lisa in our kitchen, sharing everything that had transpired from beginning to end, and then I begged for her forgiveness. Then I drove over to the church, gathered my staff, and did the same. Later that night at an emergency Leadership Team meeting, I walked our bewildered church overseers step-by-step through every detail of my secret. A few days later, standing before the church, I completely fell apart. Four long years of strategic rationalizing couldn't protect me from the inevitable—*my sin had indeed found me out.*

Do you want to know what's scary? When I confessed this, nobody really cared. In fact, the response from a man on my

Leadership Team captured the response of just about everyone: "Oh, thank God. You really scared me," he said. "I thought you called us together to tell us that you did something serious like have an affair."

Want to know what's even scarier? You probably agree with him.

I've shared that story hundreds of times over the last two decades, and each time I've always gotten the same reaction: "Let me get this straight—you started believing in hell again because you reread every passage in the New Testament that talked about hell and then fell on the ground and asked for forgiveness?"

When you put it that way, well, then yes, that's exactly how it happened. But it wasn't that simple. There was much more going on beneath the surface. Undergirding that experience were two foundational truths that I didn't come to realize until much later.

Christians must repent of "sins of disbelief" in the same way they repent of "sins of behavior."

Most Christians I know think they need to ask God's forgiveness only for things they *do* that are outside of God's will for His followers. *Did I lie today? I need to ask for forgiveness. Did I gossip? I need to ask for forgiveness for that sin too. Did I take something that wasn't mine? I'll ask for forgiveness for that as well.* Sins of disbelief are no different. 1 Timothy 4:16 says, "Watch your life and doctrine closely. Persevere in them, because if you do, you will save both yourself and your hearers."

It's life *and* doctrine—we can sin against God in both how we act *and* how we think. Both our actions and our thoughts should be under Christ's control because both have the power to negatively impact our relationship with God and the spiritual walk of everyone around us. We can't live our lives guided by the Word of God and then allow our minds to function differently. Scripture tells us to love the Lord our God with … what? All our hearts, souls, *and* minds! How we *think* is a reflection of our love for God. Don't believe me? Reread the New Testament and notice how many times the phrase *false teachers* pops up. Then look at how ruthlessly Paul and other church leaders deal with false teaching.

Christians don't think their way out of a faith crisis; they repent their way out of a faith crisis.

When it comes to leaving behind "sins of disbelief," recapturing a biblically correct position regarding the reality of hell (and the fact that non-Christians will go there) is never accomplished by laying out all the evidence and weighing the options. It's about obedience to Jesus Christ. At its core, believing in hell is an obedience issue, not a theological issue. Am I willing to trust Christ to forgive my sins? That's an obedience issue. Am I also willing to trust what He says about heaven? Of course. He's my Lord. If He says it, I believe it. Then why would the issue of hell be any different? As Oswald Chambers wrote,

> The golden rule for understanding spiritually is not intellect, but obedience. If a man wants scientific knowledge, intellectual curiosity is his guide; but if he wants insight into what Jesus Christ teaches, he can only get it by obedience. If things are dark to me, then I may be sure there is something I will not do.[12]

The fact of the matter is: *Hell is real.* Deciding whether or not hell exists isn't an intellectual exercise; it's a matter of eternal life or death.

Of course I still have doubts about hell from time to time, but the point is my relationship with the risen Jesus supersedes all my doubts. The reality you and I need to grasp is that this is happening. Right now. On our watch. This is happening to friends and acquaintances of yours and mine who aren't Christians. And you and I have one decision to make in this matter—are we going to keep on driving and pretend we know nothing, or are we going to turn around?

If you're ready to slam on the brakes and do a 180, I'll sit in the passenger's seat and take that ride with you. I'll help you understand why hell makes sense. I'll also help you feel good about believing in the Bible—*all of it*. I'll help you feel confident defending what you believe before your friends who lump you together with the crazy televangelists who make people want to throw up in their mouths. Together we'll discover that believing what the Bible teaches regarding hell is logical, fair, and above all else—*loving*.

And finally, if you let me, I'll also coach you on how you can have authentic conversations with your friends without getting creepy in the process. That's really, really important. More on that later.

However, I have one tiny piece of advice: You might want to grab a Pringles can because we're not stopping.

NOTES

1. H. Richard Niebuhr, quoted in Philip Yancey, *What's So Amazing About Grace?* (Grand Rapids, MI: Zondervan, 1997), 13–14.

2. Bill Cosby, "The Grandparents," *Himself* (Motown, 1983), compact disc.

3. Greg Garrison, "Many Americans Don't Believe in Hell, but What about Pastors?" *USA Today,* August 1, 2008, http://www.usatoday.com/news/religion/2009-08-01-Hell-damnation_N.htm.

4. Christiane Wicker, "'How Spiritual Are We?' The PARADE Spirituality Poll," *PARADE,* October 4, 2009, 5.

5. William C. Easttom II, quoted in Gary Poole, *How Could God Allow Suffering and Evil?* (Grand Rapids, MI: Zondervan, 2003), 59.

6. Tertullian, *The Apology,* quoted in Alexander Roberts and James Donaldson, trans., *Ante-Nicene Fathers* (Peabody, MA: Hendrickson, 1999), 4:52.

7. Edward T. Babinski, "Hell and Heaven, and Satan, and Christian Superstition," October 22, 2005, http://www.edwardtbabinski.us/skepticism/heaven_hell.html.

8. Victor Hugo, quoted in Rufus K. Noyes, M.D., *Views of Religion* (Boston: L.K. Washburn, 1906), 125.

9. Clark Pinnock, "The Destruction of the Finally Impenitent," *Criswell Theological Review* 4 (1990): 246–47, 253, as quoted in Randy Alcorn, *Heaven* (Carol Stream, IL: Tyndale, 2004), 24–25.

10. A. W. Tozer, *The Formula for a Burning Heart,* quoted in Martin H. Manser, compiler, *The Westminster Collection of Christian Quotations* (Louisville, KY: Westminster John Knox Press, 2001), 363.

11. See Matthew 7:21–23; 8:12; 10:15, 33; 11:22–24; 12:41–42; 13:30, 40–43, 49–50; 24:50–51; 25:11–12, 29–46.

12. Oswald Chambers, *My Utmost for His Highest* (New York: Dodd, Mead & Company, 1935), 209.

2

APOCALYPTIC URGENCY

> Most people are reached one by one, as each is made to see both the inadequacy of his own life and the glory that might come in his life if he were really to give himself fully to the cause of Jesus Christ. But we must never suggest that such discipleship is easy or mild. Everyone who enters, says Jesus, enters violently or not at all. There is no easy Christianity; there is no mild Christianity. It is violent or nothing at all.
>
> —*Elton Trueblood*[1]

Recently, I taught a four-week sermon series called "Why?" I asked people in our church to help me pick the sermon topics by sharing the "God questions" that troubled them.

Some of the questions people asked me to address were humorous:

- Why is chocolate so fattening?
- Why do I have so much hair on my back?
- Do I get to pick the dress size I'll wear in heaven?

A few of the questions were quite serious:

- Why can't I meet someone to date who's normal?
- Why is my son gay?
- Why do I struggle with depression?
- Why did God allow my brother to commit suicide?

Among all the questions people shared, someone asked this:

> I find it absolutely ridiculous to think that God would send an amazingly good person who isn't a Christian to hell. Will He do that?

The moment I read it, I loved it—the question is straight to the point—just what I've come to expect from my beloved church family. What I love about people who live in the Philadelphia metro area is their point-blank honesty (we are, after all, the same people who embrace our reputation as the only fans in the NFL ever to boo and throw snowballs at Santa Claus). The only thing more direct than the question was the response I received when I answered it in church on Sunday. Like people walking out of a bad movie, I can still picture the steady stream of confused and angry visitors getting out of their seats and walking out the exit.

Here's the question I'd like to ask you: How would you have answered that question?

As you're pondering your response, I'd like you to picture in your mind the most amazingly good person you know who isn't a Christian. Maybe that person is your parent, a family member, or a close friend. Maybe she is a remarkably kind Jewish woman who coached one of your sports teams or a profoundly spiritual but unbelieving teacher in your hometown school. Maybe he is a leader in another religious faith doing amazing things on behalf of the poor in your area. Maybe this person raises money for charities, embraces those who are discriminated against, or works tirelessly on behalf of those with disabilities. My bet is you know at least one amazingly good person who isn't a committed disciple of Jesus.

Now, ask yourself, "Given all the good this person has done, do I honestly think this person will go to hell if they don't become a Christian before they die?"

My guess is that your answer is probably no.

Or "of course not."

Or you rolled your eyes.

Or you thought, *I just can't see how a loving God would do such a thing.*

Or my personal favorite response, "This is an irrelevant question because God is the judge."

If you mulled over any of those answers in your mind, then I have two thoughts I'd like to share with you.

First, it appears you're in good company.

Second, I don't know how to say this except to just come right out and say it—you've been duped. That's right, I don't care if you have thirty-seven PhDs. You've been bamboozled, mislead, tricked, punk'd, scammed, and all the other synonyms for *deceived.* Just because you're in good company doesn't mean you're right.

To be fair, you probably answered no to that question because you are a normal, compassionate, open-minded, intelligent, and well-adjusted (okay I might be stretching things here) person who just so happens to have been born in a period of human history when tolerance of one another's religious beliefs reigns supreme.

Let's acknowledge that almost everyone thinks this way. Let's acknowledge that you're in good company. Let's even acknowledge that some churches say they believe in hell but never talk about it. But let's also acknowledge the fact that you could be wrong. Smart, well-intentioned, and sophisticated people get duped all the time. I know, because as I talked about in the previous chapter, I was duped myself.

You have this book in your hands because the time for being duped is over.

You are smart.

You can think for yourself.

And the time for allowing our twenty-first century culture to squeeze you into believing that "everyone's beliefs are equally valid" is over. That mind-set is done. As St. Chrysostom so ominously warned, "We must not mind insulting men, if by respecting them we offend God."[2]

The time to love Jesus with *all* your mind, as well as *all* your heart, is here.

It's time to get serious.

The heart of this book is about one simple idea—something I call "apocalyptic urgency." Apocalyptic urgency is the all-consuming conviction that overtakes you when you realize that hell is real, and that it is within your power to help people avoid going there.

Apocalypse is a word usually reserved to describe the cataclysmic events associated with the end of the world. In my mind, Christians focus on the wrong apocalypse. The only "apocalypse" that we can really understand and change in any way is the apocalypse awaiting every unsaved individual when he or she dies. This apocalypse is something we can predict with breathtaking accuracy. The last time I checked, the death rate for the average person was still near 100 percent. If that rate holds up, you and I can be sure that every non-Christian we lock eyes with will experience his or her own personal apocalypse.

Urgency comes as a result of what we believe about the end of human life. Hebrews 9:27 tells us, "People are destined to die once, and after that to face judgment." The Bible teaches that when people die, their eternal destiny is determined by the choice either to accept Christ as the payment for their sins, or to reject Him. Knowing this, and knowing that people within our sphere of influence need us to give them this information, creates an alarming sense of urgency.

Practically speaking, if everyone goes to heaven, why bother with Jesus at all? Why attend church? Why serve? Why tithe? Why share our faith with others? None of this makes any sense. Why would we do anything beyond that which makes us feel good? If there is no hell, then giving less than our best to our faith makes perfect sense.

But if hell is real, it changes everything. I'm convinced that if we were to truly believe in hell, there would be no cost too high, no sacrifice too great, no pain too unbearable to keep us from doing everything in our power to convince people of this reality and show them the way out. To live any other way would be unthinkable. It would be beyond immoral. It would be heinous.

The fourth-century monk St. Anthony wrote, "A time is coming when men will go mad, and when they see someone who is not mad, they will attack him saying, 'You are mad, you are not like us.'"[3]

I believe that time is now. Christians say they believe the Bible, but anyone today who takes the Bible's teaching on hell seriously is called intolerant, fanatical, and strange.

Yet, ever since that day in the monastery, I've felt this unnerving conviction that what the Bible teaches is true: Hell is real, people without Christ in their lives go there, and I have a responsibility to reach every single person within my sphere of influence before it is too late. The more I've studied the Bible, the more I've realized the apostle Paul felt the same conviction.

While talking about his heartbreak over the fact that his own people, the Jewish nation, had rejected Christ, Paul pulls back the veil of his heart to let us see what motivated him to keep sharing the gospel of Jesus in the face of extreme persecution:

> I speak the truth in Christ—I am not lying, my conscience confirms it in the Holy Spirit—I have great sorrow and unceasing anguish in my heart. For I could wish that I myself were cursed and cut off from Christ for the sake of my people, those of my own race, the people of Israel. (Rom. 9:1–4)

"Great sorrow and unceasing anguish in my heart"—that's apocalyptic urgency in a nutshell. The fact that his friends were going to hell physically affected him. He couldn't go about his daily routine as if this didn't bother him. Actually, their lost state before God didn't just bother him; *it consumed him*. Paul didn't feel sorrow, but "great sorrow." He didn't feel anguish, but "unceasing anguish." William Sanday captures the intensity of Paul's thought when he translates

Romans 9:2: "There is one grief I cannot shake off, one distressing weight that lies forever at my heart."[4]

Here's my question: How about you? Do you feel great sorrow and unceasing anguish for that non-Christian friend you work with? That Jewish neighbor? That Hindu person who works at the restaurant you frequent? If not, why not? To me there are only two answers to that question: You either don't believe in hell, or you don't care that your friends will go there when they die. There's no middle ground here. Most Christians I meet either don't believe that their non-Christian friends are going to hell, or worse, don't care. Either way, they can't point to a time in their lives when they've felt "great sorrow and unceasing anguish in their hearts" (v. 2) for their nonbelieving friends. Are you one of them?

Robert Ingersoll, a famous nineteenth-century atheist, wrote,

> If there is a God who will damn his children forever, I would rather go to hell than to go to heaven and keep the society of such an infamous tyrant. … I do not believe this doctrine; neither do you. If you did, you could not sleep one moment. Any man who believes it, and has within his breast a decent, throbbing heart, will go insane. A man who believes that doctrine and does not go insane has the heart of a snake, and the conscience of a hyena.[5]

At least Ingersoll got one thing right—hell isn't something you can be ambivalent about. What I take exception to is not the intensity with which Ingersoll characterizes a life lived believing in hell, rather the source of that intensity. It's not insanity that drives us to reach out to those going to hell, but love. Love compels us. Love drives us. Love causes us to risk friendships, relationships, business partnerships, and whatever else stands in the way to help people come to a saving relationship with Jesus Christ.

Common sense tells me that if I truly believed that people who die without Christ will spend not just one year, or 150 years, or 150,000 years, or 150 trillion years, but an *eternity* in hell, this would be a game-changer. I would completely upend my life in the pursuit of changing the course of every person I met. Everything about me would change—the way I spend my time, the way I spend my money, my career choices, activities my kids get involved in, my priorities, my daily schedule, everything. If my life truly reflected what I say I believe, everything about my life would change.

The need to evangelize is so self-evident that even people who aren't Christians realize it. Comedian and spiritual skeptic Penn Jillette posed a question that I think every Christian must answer:

> I don't respect people who don't proselytize. If you believe there is a heaven and a hell and people could be going to hell … and you think it's not worth telling them this because it would make it socially awkward … how much do you have to hate someone to not proselytize? How much do you have to hate someone to believe everlasting life is possible and not tell them that?[6]

Apocalyptic urgency is what drove the great Christian missionaries and martyrs of the past to sacrifice personal ambition, comfort, and security to advance the message of Jesus. And my prayer is that as you read the following chapters, apocalyptic urgency will overtake you as well. *It must.* Too much is riding on this for even one person to succumb to a life of self-centered apathy. My prayer is for God to so disturb you by what you read in the following pages that it will be impossible for your life to go back to the way you lived it before.

URGENT LOVE

In the next chapter, I'll begin exploring the main reasons people like you and I lose a sense of apocalyptic urgency. But before I do that, there is one more person I would like you to bring to mind. You are sitting across from that amazingly good person you know who isn't a Christian; now I'd like you to imagine Jesus. Picture this good person staring straight ahead; now picture Jesus as He looks into this person's eyes. What kind of look does He have on His face? What emotion can you read in His body language? What is He thinking as He looks at this person who is preparing to die and face eternal condemnation because he or she didn't place faith in Him?

Fortunately, we don't have to guess what this picture might look like. Second Peter 3:8 tells us, "But do not forget this one thing, dear friends: With the Lord a day is like a thousand years, and a thousand years are like a day." When Peter penned these words, the apostles were dying. People began to question whether or not Jesus would actually return as He promised. So the apostle Peter reassured his readers that God's view of time is not our own. Even though fifty, two hundred, or five thousand years may pass between Christ's life on earth and His actual return, "a thousand years are like a day" to God.

Unfortunately, we typically miss half the meaning of that verse. Not only are we meant to refrain from being discouraged at any seeming delay of Christ's coming, we're also meant to remember that "with the Lord a day is like a thousand years." But we typically skip that first part.

I know what it's like to sit outside waiting for my daughters to finish soccer practice. Sometimes an extra ten minutes can seem like an hour. I've had to wait an extra thirty or forty minutes before. When my other kids need to be picked up and dinner needs to be made, waiting an extra thirty or forty minutes can seem like two hours. I'm sure you can relate. In this verse Peter tells us that when God waits not thirty minutes but a whole day, that whole day can feel like a thousand years. Why would one twenty-four hour day *feel* like a thousand years to God? I think the answer is obvious. As the New Testament scholar Michael Green observes, "God sees time with an *intensity* we lack; one day with the Lord is like a thousand years."[7]

As time rushes toward an irreversible climax, and Jesus sees His followers miss opportunity after opportunity to reach the people for whom He died, each day must literally feel like a thousand years. He must feel like the family member waiting for news from the operating room about a loved one clinging to life, as time stands still. Knowing what is at stake, that two-minute conversation you had today with the coworker who hasn't become a Christian yet must have felt like an hour to God. Each word, the weight of the opportunity, the high-stakes drama unfolding before His eyes—it must have been unbearable. The sheer urgency of His love for that person must consume Him.

I asked you to picture Jesus and your amazingly good friend together for this reason: Either this is an accurate representation of what is really going on—or this whole concept of God, Jesus, hell, and eternity is a ridiculously cruel lie, and I'm the one who's really been duped.

NOTES

1. Elton Trueblood, *The Yoke of Christ* (Waco, TX: Word Books, 1958), 89.

2. St. John Chrysostom, *Six Books on the Priesthood,* trans. Graham Neville (Crestwood, NY: St. Vladimir's Seminary Press, 1977), 65.

3. St. Anthony, *Sayings of the Desert Fathers,* trans. Benedicta Ward (Kalamazoo, MI: Cistercian Publications, 1975), 7.

4. William Sanday, *The Epistle to the Romans* (New York: Charles Scribner's Sons, 1929), 225.

5. Robert G. Ingersoll, *Works of Robert Ingersoll* (New York: Bibliobazaar, 2007), 182.

6. Penn Jillette, "A Gift of a Bible," *Crackle* video 5:00, December 9, 2008, http://crackle.com/c/Penn_Says/A_Gift_of_a_Bible/2415037.

7. Michael Green, *2 Peter & Jude* (Grand Rapids, MI: Eerdmans, 1987), 146.

PART TWO

IF HELL IS REAL ... WHY AM I AFRAID TO ADMIT IT?

3

ASHAMED

When it comes to bull——, big-time, major-league bull—— you have to stand in awe of the all-time champion of false promises and exaggerated claims—religion.

—George Carlin[1]

I hold the distinct honor of being the only pastor in two thousand years of church history ever to sucker punch a spiritual skeptic in the middle of an evangelistic conversation.

A few months ago a friend of mine asked me what my next book was going to be about. I told him it was going to be a book about hell. I told him about how most Christians don't believe in it any longer, and how if they did, it would forever change the way they interact with the people around them who aren't followers of Jesus.

No response. He just stood there silently.

"Well? Aren't you going to say something?"

"You mean you want me to tell you want I think of that?" he responded.

"Well, yes. What do you think?" I said.

"We're friends, so I'm just going be honest," he said. "Do you realize how whacked-out that sounds? Don't be offended, but that's just not normal." He continued, "Let me put it this way: On a crazy meter—with one being the Amish and a ten being those polygamous alien abduction nuts living in communes in the desert of New Mexico—what you just told me is, well, that's, like, a twelve."

"Oh, shut up, it is not," I shot back. "It's orthodox Christian belief clearly taught in the Bible."

"I don't care what you call it—it's seriously messed up," he replied.

"It is not. Every Bible-believing church teaches this. In fact, that Catholic church you take your kids to—the one you only attend on Christmas and Easter—they believe this too."

"But I don't believe a thing they teach."

"Oh, that's great. You absolutely insist that your kids go there for CCD classes, but you don't believe anything they teach. And you're calling me whacked-out?"

"Brian, here's what I don't get—you're, like, normal. You're smart. You have a great family. You're a pretty cool guy to hang out with. But now I find out you've got this crazy way of viewing me, and people like me who aren't Christians. That's just messed up ..."

And that's when it happened.

Just as the words *messed up* left his lips, something inside of me snapped, and I freaked out. Without thinking, I threw an explosive sucker punch to his gut, instantly dropping him to his knees.

I leaned over and slowly whispered in his ear, "Don't you *ever* talk to me like that again. How's that for being messed up?"

Then I walked away in disgust.

And that's when it hit me—I had just single-handedly delivered the greatest pastoral butt kicking in the history of, um, *my imagination*.

That's because I didn't actually hit him.

I wanted to.

Believe me, I wanted to.

But I didn't.

Instead, I let his demeaning words just sit in the air.

When it got too awkward to no longer respond, I halfheartedly cracked a joke.

"Wanna know what's *really* messed up?"

"What?"

"Your face."

He kind of laughed. And I sort of smiled. Then he said, "Hey, I've got to run," with an awkward "I'm leaving now and our relationship is never going to be quite the same" look in his eye.

And I felt small.

And ashamed.

And stupid.

And judgmental.

And alone.

WHY CHRISTIANS LOSE APOCALYPTIC URGENCY

For the next three chapters I want to explore why Christians stop believing in hell. What I felt during that conversation—that awkward sense of alienation and shame twisting my insides—that's the first reason. Christians stop believing in hell because they allow the non-Christians around them to make them feel stupid for believing in it. In my experience, followers of Jesus can go in the blink of an eye from wholeheartedly believing in the need to save their friends from hell to believing "everybody goes to heaven" all because of something a non-Christian said to them. This has been going on for two thousand years.

I want to help change that.

THE POWER OF AN INSULT

Throughout its history, the church has made a big deal about how things like sexual sin, power, and greed derail the urgency and effectiveness of radically sold-out followers of Jesus. While I'm not going to try to dispute the claims of historians and theologians much smarter than myself, I would like to add a fourth reason to their list—*embarrassment*. In my experience as a pastor, plain and simple embarrassment has done more to derail the evangelistic passion of Christ followers than the other three combined.

Simply put, most Christians are too embarrassed to believe in hell. At least with the pitfalls of money, sex, and power, the cause of the temptation and the cure both come from the same source—*the Christian's own heart*.

But embarrassment is another story. Embarrassment stems from the need for anyone, not just Christians, to feel accepted and loved by friends and family. In fact, our longing for acceptance is much more powerful than our desire for money, sex, or power. I've met lots of poor people who are happy. I know many who are perfectly content without power. I have friends who are perfectly satisfied living a life of complete celibacy. But I've never met a person who is happy, yet feels unloved.

Acceptance takes two people, and it can be both extended and withheld. It is something that is largely out of our control, and therein lies the problem for the Christian. Acceptance and embarrassment go hand in hand. Lack of one produces the other. Show me someone who doesn't feel accepted by those around them, and I'll show you someone who feels too embarrassed to openly embrace what he or she really believes.

The problem is that a Christian who believes in hell and believes people who don't accept Jesus will go there for eternity is never going to be accepted by his or her non-Christian friends. It's just not going to happen. Let's be honest—hell isn't one of those topics of conversation that gets us invited back to dinner parties. We're never going to have a conversation with a non-Christian over Chicken Cordon Bleu after which he will lean over and tell us, "You know, I just love it when you insinuate that I'm going to hell. Love it. Love it. *Love it.*"

Jesus warns us that if we truly believe what He teaches and live the life He calls us to live, the non-Christians around us won't accept us:

> You will be hated by everyone because of me. (Matt. 10:22)

> You will be hated by all nations because of me. (Matt. 24:9)

> If the world hates you, keep in mind that it hated me first. (John 15:18)

Two thousand years of church history have validated Jesus' claims. Read any history book if you doubt His comments. Turn on any late-night talk show. Or flip on the radio. Our culture ridicules

Christians who take the Bible seriously and calls them Jesus freaks. There's a reason the apostle Peter warned, "Do not be surprised at the fiery ordeal that has come on you to test you, as though something strange were happening to you" (1 Peter 4:12). If you truly live out your beliefs, non-Christians are going to think you're nuts. And they will tell you so. *To your face*. A lot.

The only comforting thing about this is that it's nothing new. It's been going on for two thousand years.

FIRST-CENTURY INSULTS

Take the book of Hebrews, for example. We don't know a lot about the person who wrote it or the people who received it other than what we can discern from contextual clues. As we read the book, the first thing we discover is that the Christians who received the letter had once been valiant in the face of extreme persecution. Their plight gives us a first-hand look at the intense social pressure first-century Christians faced.

> Remember those earlier days after you had received the light, when you endured in a great conflict full of suffering. (Heb. 10:32)

> You suffered along with those in prison and joyfully accepted the confiscation of your property, because you knew that you yourselves had better and lasting possessions. (v. 34)

But despite their long-standing history of bravery in the face of unrelenting community pressure, something changed. Something caused them to lose their zeal; so much so that many of them stopped gathering together as believers.

> And let us consider how we may spur one another on toward love and good deeds, not giving up meeting together, as some are in the habit of doing. (vv. 24–25)

How did this happen? How did these Christians go from letting unbelievers confiscate their property just to show them that their faith was real to skipping church and watching TV evangelists? Something powerful and disturbing must have happened in their community. To me the culprit is found in one lethal word: *insult*.

> Sometimes you were publicly exposed to *insult* and persecution. (v. 33)

The Christians addressed in the book of Hebrews could have been worn down by physical persecution—punches, torturing, etc. That's a distinct possibility. We weren't there, so we'll never know for sure. But my money is on the fact that it was the *ridicule* they faced day in and day out that slowly caused them to throw their confidence away (v. 35). One little insult attached itself to another, then another, and over time, like the breaching of a dam, their certainty crumbled under the pressure. New Testament scholar David deSilva describes the situation these believers faced: "The Christians' neighbors had attempted to shame the deviants back into conformity."[2] Whatever they said and did worked.

The word our English Bibles translate as "insult" is the Greek verb *oneidizō,* which means "to revile, reproach, or disgrace." In some instances it means "to behave childishly,"[3] which underscores why being insulted can be a deceptive experience. Unlike maturely airing differences and attempting to come to a rational, amicable solution, insults are time-delayed, hit-and-run assaults. Generally, we don't realize the toll they've taken until much later when we've had a chance to process our emotions. By that time the damage has already been done. Insults make us feel small, ashamed, and stupid. They're corrosive to the soul. It's understandable why Jesus and other early church leaders tried to encourage first-century disciples by getting them to re-envision insults as blessings in disguise:

> *Blessed* are you when people *insult* (*oneidizō)* you, persecute you and falsely say all kinds of evil against you because of me. (Matt. 5:11)

> *Blessed* are you when people hate you, when they exclude you and *insult* (*oneidizō)* you and reject your name as evil, because of the Son of Man. (Luke 6:22)

> If you are *insulted* (*oneidizō)* because of the name of Christ, you are *blessed*, for the Spirit of glory and of God rests on you. (1 Peter 4:14)

This much is clear: If you believe in hell, you will pay a price. But chances are good that most of us aren't going to be beaten or spit upon. People will, however, make us feel like dim-witted and judgmental losers. Insults are inevitable. People insulted Jesus. People insulted His followers. People insulted the Christians in the churches established by the apostles. And people will insult you. Steady yourself. "Be strong in the Lord and in his mighty power," Paul encouraged. "Put on the full armor of God, so that you can take your stand against the devil's schemes" (Eph. 6:10–11). Insults are the Enemy's primary weapon. His target is your confidence. The spoils of his victory will be the souls of your non-Christian friends, the very people he's using to insult you.

SECOND-CENTURY INSULTS

Unfortunately, insults against Christians continued well into the second century. For example, sometime in the second century a philosopher named Celsus became the first non-Christian to ever take Christianity seriously enough to write a book against it. His comments were brutal. Celsus's book, *The True Word*, was lost over time, but large excerpts of his work were preserved by a third-century pastor named Origen in his book *Against Celsus*. This non-Christian philosopher's vitriolic words give us insight into the kinds of insults leveled against second-century Christ followers.

Notice how Celsus accused Christians of only encouraging the unintelligent to join their ranks:

> The following are the rules laid down by them. Let no one come to us who has been instructed, or who is wise or prudent (for such qualifications are

> deemed evil by us); but if there be any ignorant, or unintelligent, or uninstructed, or foolish persons, let them come with confidence.[4]

Taking his attack against the intelligence of Christians even further, Celsus argued that Christians never discuss their beliefs with those more educated than themselves:

> We see, indeed, in private houses workers in wool and leather, and fullers, and persons of the most uninstructed and rustic character, not venturing to utter a word in the presence of their elders and wiser masters; but when they get hold of the children privately, and certain women as ignorant as themselves, they pour forth wonderful statements.[5]

While Origen went to great lengths to demonstrate otherwise, Celsus argued that this new religion could not be trusted because it was a faith comprised of ignorant fools:

> Only foolish and low individuals, and persons devoid of perception, and slaves, and women, and children, of whom the teachers of the divine word wish to make converts.[6]

Finally, his contempt for Christians was so strong, Celsus compared Christian gatherings to …

> a flight of bats or to a swarm of ants issuing out of their nest, or to frogs holding council in a marsh, or to worms crawling together in the corner of a dunghill.[7]

Those are heavy insults—fools, devoid of perception; ignorant, unintelligent; flight of bats; swarm of ants; frogs; worms crawling to the corner of a dunghill.

No wonder Origen felt compelled to write a book against Celsus's derisive attacks. If I had my friends call me those kinds of names because I bore the name of Christ, I would've been tempted to back off my beliefs too. I'm human. I know how words like that, especially over time, take a toll.

For two thousand years Christians have struggled with non-Christians who made them feel small and alone. The thing is, we've never been alone. Not only do we have a "great cloud of witnesses" (Heb. 12:1) cheering us on, but Jesus Himself is with us. "Consider him," the writer of Hebrews wrote, "who endured such opposition from sinners, so that you will not grow weary and lose heart" (v. 3).

Origen knew the scornful words of non-Christians like Celsus could potentially leave deep scars on the hearts of his fellow Christians. That's why in another book, *Exhortation to Martyrdom,* he encouraged Christians to pray the following prayer whenever they felt like giving up:

> It is probable that we shall be insulted by our neighbors, and certain people we associate with will turn up their noses and shake their heads at us as

> though we were mad. When this happens, let us say to God: … *All these things have come upon us, yet we have not forgotten Thee … our heart hath not turned back.* [8]

I've lost track of the number of times conversations with non-Christians have left me feeling stupid. I'll even question whether or not I've been deluded into believing some jacked-up way of viewing the universe and the non-Christians around me. Oftentimes I'll nod my head and think to myself, *Maybe he's right. Maybe I am whacked-out. Maybe I am seriously messed up in the head. Maybe everybody goes to heaven regardless of his or her faith, and I'm inviting ridicule for nothing.*

But when that happens, something deep inside of me always brings Jesus to mind. It's weird. Like Origen instructed, I'll force myself not to allow the insults to cause me to forget what Jesus went through for me. I'll remember that I'm not the only one to be insulted—as Jesus hung in agony on the cross "those who passed by hurled insults at him" (Mark 15:29). I'll bring to mind His words, "If the world hates you, keep in mind that it hated me first" (John 15:18).

Then I'll calm myself and pray Origen's simple prayer: "Jesus, I will not turn back." Sometimes I'll have to repeat this over and over again, but eventually I regain my perspective.

THIRD-CENTURY INSULTS

There's one more exceptionally cruel example I'd like to share. This anti-Christian slur comes not from a book but from a piece of graffiti dated sometime in the third century. In 1857, archaeologists discovered a drawing that had been scratched onto the wall of an army guardroom on Palatine Hill near the Circus Maximus in Rome. The *Alexamenos Graffito,* as it is called, gives us an example of the negative social pressure that the disciples of Jesus faced well into the third century.[9]

The exact details surrounding the creation of the graffito are guesswork, but this much we can surmise from the piece of graffiti itself: There was a Christian man named Alexamenos who served as a Roman guard stationed in Rome. The soldiers around him knew he was a Christian. At some point it appears that one of his fellow guards grabbed a knife and scratched this picture on the wall of the guardroom.

The details of the picture are hard to make out, so I've traced the drawing here.[10]

On the left stands a man with his arm raised in the air, as if praying or worshipping. At the top of the drawing is a cross. Hanging on the cross is a crucified man with the head of a donkey. Scratched at the bottom are the Greek words:

ALE
XAMENOS
SEBETE
THEON

Translation: "Alexamenos worships (his) god."

Let that comment sink in for a moment.

Imagine the laughs Alexamenos heard when he walked back into his guardroom and discovered the picture. Think about what he sensed at that moment—*feel that*. Think about the sense of shame and apprehension he must have felt inside—I've felt that before, especially when the topic of hell has come up. Maybe you have too. Maybe you felt it when someone made a snide comment about Christianity at work. Maybe you felt it when you walked in the door after church and your non-Christian spouse made a hurtful comment about your faith. Maybe you felt it as you walked down the hallway at school and overheard your friends talking about your faith behind your back.

For two thousand years Christians have felt immense pressure to give up their beliefs because of the insults they faced. Christians have received high marks on the crazy meter in every century since Christ walked the earth.

Embarrassment is nothing new for the Christian.

Fortunately, neither is the cure.

NOT ASHAMED

The apostle Paul boldly declared in Romans 1:16–17, "I am not ashamed of the gospel." That's quite an understatement. If ever there was someone who wasn't deterred by insults and persecution, it was Paul. The lengths to which he and his band of followers went in order to spread the gospel are unparalleled.

> To this very hour we go hungry and thirsty, we are in rags, we are brutally treated, we are homeless.

> We work hard with our own hands. When we are cursed, we bless; when we are persecuted, we endure it; when we are slandered, we answer kindly. We have become the scum of the earth, the garbage of the world—right up to this moment. (1 Cor. 4:11–13)

In fact, the legacy of the apostle Paul's life is staggering—he established hundreds of churches; raised up and commissioned countless church planters; wrote thirteen letters in the Bible; and single-handedly catapulted Christianity on a trajectory that would eventually lead it to become the largest religion in the Mediterranean world. Simply put, there has never been a more influential Christ follower.

But there's always one aspect of Paul's story that many historians and biblical scholars leave off his list of accomplishments, and that's his time as a confused truth seeker. Not long after his conversion, the apostle Paul "went into Arabia" (Gal. 1:17). It was there, where he spent a few years before his high-profile ministry began, that he wasn't confident about anything. How do we know this? Because Paul was an expert on the Old Testament, but beyond that he was a theological blank slate. He knew nothing! Ransacked by the risen Jesus, Paul had to construct his understanding of Christianity from the ground up. There was no textbook he could consult, and he purposely chose not to have contact with any of the apostles during this time.

What this means is that Paul didn't become a Christian and instantly become an apocalyptically urgent believer. It took him time to wrap his head around who Jesus was, the meaning of His death and resurrection for the world, and why he'd been called to reach people separated from God. Sure, Paul was a driven person right after his conversion. He was a type A personality before and after coming to Christ. But personality alone doesn't make someone apocalyptically urgent. Calm, introverted people can live with staggering levels of passion to reach their friends for Christ. Apocalyptic urgency comes from a place of deep assurance about what you believe and what you're being called to do. At that time, Paul had neither.

Paul still had to ponder the nature of heaven and the existence of hell. He had to let God show him everything. There were no teachers, no Christian books, and no New Testament Scriptures (he hadn't written them yet). All Paul had were the Old Testament Scriptures and a well-worn spot on the ground where he met the risen Jesus in prayer.

I find Paul's searching phase incredibly encouraging. I didn't instantly become convinced about the reality of hell either. It took time. I had to process it. It was the prototypical "three steps forward, two steps back" journey. There were even conversations that put me four steps back. I had to believe it, reject it, and then come back to it again.

Paul asked his questions, aired his doubts, and the Holy Spirit answered him while he was alone in the desert of Arabia. "I want you to know," Paul proclaimed, "that the gospel I preached is not of human origin. I did not receive it from any man, nor was I taught it; rather, I received it by revelation from Jesus Christ" (Gal. 1:11–12). That must have been an intellectually turbulent time of discovery for Paul. I know it was for me. I'm fairly certain it was, or will be, for you, too.

Paul went into the desert a man full of questions and emerged a few years later a man on a mission.

Here's my question about that time: What happened? What did Paul discover? New Testament scholar C. E .B. Cranfield states, "The gospel is something of which, in this world, Christians will constantly be tempted to be ashamed."[11] What was revealed to Paul about the gospel that had the opposite effect on him?

Paul discovered three spiritual truths during those years in Arabia that so profoundly impacted his thinking that they carried him through thirty years of suffering and eventual martyrdom for Christ.

These truths will create a sense of boldness in us like no other.

TRUTHS THAT GENERATE BOLDNESS

1. Non-Christians Won't Fully "Get It" until After Conversion

Paul wrote in 1 Corinthians 2:14, "The person without the Spirit does not accept the things that come from the Spirit of God but considers them foolishness, and cannot understand them because they are discerned only through the Spirit."

What he means is that there are certain spiritual truths that will never make sense to people until *after* conversion. We are never going to be in a position where we talk with a non-Christian and he or she responds, "You know, this hell business makes perfect sense to me. Thanks for sharing." Why? Because believing the basic truths of Christianity takes more than cognitive processing; it requires the power of God's Spirit to soften the will and emotions. Without God's Spirit softening the heart, non-Christians will never want to "see" truths that can only be understood or appreciated with the "eyes of your heart" (Eph. 1:18).

G. K. Chesterton wrote, "A man cannot think himself out of mental evil; for it is actually the organ of thought that has become diseased, ungovernable, and, as it were, independent. He can only be saved by will or faith."[12] Paul knew this firsthand. He himself had spewed insults against the very Christians who were trying to reach him. "Even though I was once a blasphemer and a persecutor and a violent man," Paul wrote, "I was shown mercy because I acted in ignorance and unbelief" (1 Tim. 1:13).

Knowing this, Paul never really seemed bothered by the insults hurled at him by non-Christians. He understood that "the message of the cross is foolishness to those who are perishing" (1 Cor. 1:18). In the same way that parents don't allow themselves to be deterred by their children's complaints about a proper bedtime and a healthy diet, Paul knew that non-Christians' insults came from a place of ignorance.

If anything, insults motivated Paul to push harder to reach those attacking him.

2. Evangelism and Insults Always Go Hand in Hand

"I will stay on at Ephesus until Pentecost," Paul wrote, "because a great door for effective work has opened to me, and there are many who oppose me" (1 Cor. 16:8–9). Open doors for evangelism and opposition from non-Christians always go together. Paul understood that the presence of opposition was a sign that work needed to be done, not that the work he did was inappropriate.

I need to hear this.

I don't know about you, but the first thing I feel when someone insults my faith is guilt, as if I'm doing something wrong. It's a default reaction I have. Maybe it's all my years of getting ticked off at pushy telemarketers calling my house, but I don't want to seem like a pushy Christian selling something someone doesn't want to buy.

This is something we all have to move beyond emotionally. No one likes being disliked (unless you're a Yankees fan), but we're talking about life and death here. If you're pushing widgets on the phone, you should feel guilty for interrupting someone's dinner. But if you're an ambulance driver and you can't find the home of a heart attack victim who needs to go to the hospital, the last thing you should feel guilt over is calling around to find the right house.

We've been called to offer people something infinitely more important than medical assistance—it's the Word of Life, salvation, and eternal truth. Heaven and hell hang in the balance. The prospect of someone going to hell is worth taking emotional hits. Frankly, the salvation of our non-Christian friends is more important than being liked by them. We have to reconcile our minds to the reality that if we are faithful to Christ's call, some people just aren't going to like us.

Jesus had realistic expectations for what His followers would face as they attempted to spread the message of the Christian faith:

> Do not suppose that I have come to bring peace to the earth. I did not come to bring peace, but a sword. For I have come to turn "a man against his father, a daughter against her mother, a daughter-in-law against her mother-in-law—a man's enemies will be the members of his own household." (Matt. 10:34–36)

Even though Jesus used hyperbole in these verses—exaggerating for effect—the underlying truth remains. Being an apocalyptically urgent Christian is not easy. In fact, just to make sure people understood the demands of this life, Jesus clarified His point even further:

> Anyone who loves their father or mother more than me is not worthy of me; anyone who loves their son or daughter more than me is not worthy of me. Whoever does not take up their cross and follow me is not worthy of me. Whoever finds their life will lose it, and whoever loses their life for my sake will find it. (vv. 37–39)

The point here is clear—reaching out to our friends and family with the love and message of Christ is risky. Doing so may disrupt and maybe even end our relationships. Not because Jesus is calling us to be obnoxious Christians, but because some will not be open to His message, no matter how lovingly we present it.

3. Insults Now, Thanks Later

Finally, the third thing Paul learned in that Arabian desert is that those we evangelize will at some point thank us for our efforts. The apostle Paul owed his eternal salvation to a man named Stephen. Acts 7 records how Stephen boldly proclaimed his faith as Paul stood by and "approved of their killing him" (Acts 8:1).

Stephen knew that Paul might stone him in this life but thank him in the next.

Over the years I've helped hundreds of people come to faith in Christ. Many of them ridiculed me in the process, sometimes ruthlessly. But I persisted the best I could. I even hated some of them. I know that's not something I'm supposed to say as a pastor, but it's what I felt at the time. Some of the people I reached out to treated me like garbage. But somehow I persisted. And do you know what many of those same people told me *after* they became Christians?

"Thank you for not giving up on me."

Years ago a woman in our church asked me to visit her dying father in the hospital. For years this man had rejected Christianity and even made fun of me personally. But despite my years of built-up apprehension and animosity toward this man, I went to see him.

When I arrived in his room, I found a different man from the one I'd known. Gone was the bravado. Gone was the glare of defiance I had seen so many times. Hooked to a dozen wires and monitors, the person who spent a lifetime rejecting his daughter's attempts to share her faith now lay in cold silence staring out the window.

For some reason, I expected the circumstances of our meeting to have softened his heart. Deathbeds have a way of doing that to people. But as I drilled down in our conversation, I hit the same skeptical bedrock I had before. He gave me the same smirks. Same defiance. Same "I'm smarter than God" attitude. My job was done. He was unmoved and unwilling to talk about spiritual matters, so I said a quick prayer and headed for the parking lot. But something wouldn't allow me to get on that elevator.

This isn't a game, I thought. *This person is headed toward eternal separation from God.*

And you're going to just walk away and leave?

What are you ashamed of?

The elevator door opened, but I didn't get in.

Prompted by the Holy Spirit, I turned around, headed back down the hallway, and walked up to his bedside once again.

"I'm not leaving you like this. Not today. Not on my watch."

He was taken aback.

"Listen, I don't care that you've spent your life making fun of Christians. I don't care about anything you've said or done up to this point. Quite frankly, I think all of that has been a show. I can see it in your eyes. Deep down you want to believe, you just haven't been willing to humble yourself."

I spent the next fifteen minutes trying every angle possible to get him to surrender his heart to Christ. No luck. I don't know what I expected—maybe the gates of heaven to open up and shower angel dust all over the room, I don't know. All I knew is that this guy's heart wouldn't budge.

Then I did something I had never done before.

I begged him.

I literally began begging him to come to Christ.

"Look, is this what you want? I'm begging you, Frank. I'm literally begging you. You're going to die soon, maybe today, maybe tomorrow, I don't know when, but it's soon. I don't want you to go to hell. I'm begging you to give your life to Christ, right now, this second."

Then something astonishing happened. His eyes started to water. His lips trembled. Years of skeptical defiance melted as he grabbed my hand. And that's when it happened—*he surrendered his heart to Christ.*

Right there in that room.

After years of hurling insults at Christians.

And as I stood there, wiping back tears of joy and trying to figure out how I was going to baptize him with all those wires sticking out of him, he pulled my hand and motioned with his eyes that he wanted to say something.

I leaned over to listen.

And he whispered in my ear, "Thank you for coming back for me."

As we both sat there, soaking in the magnitude of what was taking place, I started laughing, wiped my eyes, and said, "Frank, after everything you've put me through, I don't know whether I should hug you or sucker punch you."

NOTES

1. George Carlin, quoted in Robin Ince, "Obituary," *New Humanist*, July/August, 2008, 23.

2. David A. deSilva, *Perseverance in Gratitude: A Socio-Rhetorical Commentary on the Epistle "to the Hebrews"* (Grand Rapids, MI: Eerdmans, 2000), 359.

3. Colin Brown, ed., *The New International Dictionary of New Testament Theology* (Grand Rapids, MI: Regency Reference Library, 1986), 3:340.

4. Origen, *Against Celsus*, trans. Alexander Roberts and James Donaldson, *Ante-Nicene Fathers* (Peabody, MA: Hendrickson,1999), 4:481–82 .

5. Ibid, 486.

6. Ibid, 484.

7. Ibid, 506.

8. Origen, *Prayer and Exhortation to Martyrdom*, trans. John J. O'Meara (New York: Newman, 1954), 160.

9. Evert Ferguson, *Backgrounds of Early Christianity* (Grand Rapids, MI: Eerdmans, 1989), 475.

10. First image from Rodolfo Lanciani, *Ancient Rome in the Light of Recent Discoveries* (New York: Houghton Mifflin: 1888), 123. (Second image traced by author.)

11. C. E .B. Cranfield, *Romans: A Shorter Commentary* (Grand Rapids, MI: Eerdmans, 1985), 17.

12. G. K. Chesterton, *Orthodoxy* (New York: Doubleday, 2001), 16.

4
DECEIVED

Nothing is more perilous than to be weary of the Word of God. Thinking he knows enough, a person begins little by little to despise the Word until he has lost Christ and the gospel altogether.

—*Martin Luther*[1]

Church planters know that you only get one guarantee when you start a new church: At some point in the first five years every nutty Christian within twenty miles will visit your services. One day, for no apparent reason, someone will get a signal from the mothership to turn off the Christian television station, put their thirty-seven cats in the basement, throw on their favorite "1 cross + 3 nails = 4 given" T-shirt, hop into a car plastered with several "In Case of Rapture This Car Will Have No Driver" bumper stickers, and head on over to check you out.

Sometimes they all show up on the same day.

I'll never forget the day years ago when a few of these lovely Christians stood in a line to talk with me after the service. The first person, a lady in her midforties, was obviously agitated.

"You mentioned in your sermon that the Christmas Eve service next week would be over in time for, and I quote, 'Santa Claus to visit the little children.'"

"Yeah, since our new church meets in a movie theater the people will be here late tearing down after the service. That was basically code to let parents know they'll still have enough time to get home and wrap presents."

"Well, you do know Satan is *in* Santa, don't you?"

"Uh … excuse me?"

"Satan is *in* Santa."

"I don't understand."

Growing more aggravated, she yelled, "I *said,* Satan is *IN* Santa. Santa is *IN* Satan. Do you get it now?"

"Uh, no, I'm afraid I don't."

"When you mentioned Santa Claus, you were actually telling people that Satan was coming, because the letters S-A-N-T-A are the same letters used to spell S-A-T-A-N."

Looking around for the closest person on our security team, I smiled and said, "Well, alrighty then, thanks for sharing that."

As I turned to the next person in line, I prayed, *God, please let this person be normal. Is that too much to ask?*

No such luck.

A woman carrying a large black Bible pushed her finger into my chest and said, "You said in your sermon that if you want to know what a Pharisee is, just picture Rush Limbaugh wearing a yarmulke."

"Yes, that was a joke. I'm sorry if that offended you."

"Oh, you better believe I was offended. Rush Limbaugh is an evangelical Christian."

"I wasn't aware of that," I replied. "I'm fairly certain though that Limbaugh doesn't claim to be an evangelical Christian."

"Well, you're right, he doesn't. But he's a Christian. He just doesn't know it."

"He's a Christian and he *doesn't even know it?*" I repeated slowly. "Uh, I'm not sure I know how that works."

"I just don't think you should slam his radio ministry."

"Ministry? He's not even a Christian, let alone a pastor."

"But people are coming to Christ listening to his radio program!"

"Listen. I'm sorry. We have to be out of here in five minutes. I don't have time to argue. We obviously have very different ways of looking at reality. So let's just agree to disagree."

She stormed off.

Behind her stood a man with a huge smile on his face.

"Great service today!" he said. "I was wondering if you had time to talk. I'd like to know how to become a Christian."

I yelled, "Yes!" and hugged him.

"What did I do?" he asked.

"Oh, nothing. God just answered a prayer of mine. How can I help?"

"The world is so cruel," he told me."I want to believe in God. I want to believe in everything you're talking about. But I can't. People are so cruel. Look at how people treat one another at work. Just look at the way people drive—cutting people off and screaming at each other in traffic—I just can't believe God would create a place like this.

"Look," I said as I checked the time on the clock. "I really hate to do this, but we've got to be out of here in four minutes flat. And then I have to race over to a baptism service we're having at a local apartment complex swimming pool. I can see God is really working in your heart. Can I give you directions to the baptism service? We can talk after that. Will that work?"

"Absolutely. I'll meet you there," he said.

I walked him to the lobby, quickly introduced him to my wife on the way out, and ducked back into the theater to finish tearing down. As I hopped into the car with my wife and three daughters, I knew I was going to be late to the baptism service.

"How did teaching your class go today?" I asked Lisa as I whipped through the parking lot like I was on the tea cup ride at Disney World.

"Great, we had six new kids. How did 'big church' go?"

"The service went great, except for the two nuts that accosted me after the service."

Suddenly, traffic slowed down. It was obvious someone was blocking the intersection ahead.

"I can't believe I'm going to be late," I said.

"Relax. We'll get there when we get there."

"I told people twelve forty-five p.m. Everyone's going to be in the water waiting for me."

I slammed my fist on the horn.

"What's taking so long at the light?" I yelled to no one in particular.

"Dad, where are we going to eat after the baptism service?" one of my daughters yelled from the backseat.

"Can't talk now. Some idiot up there in the middle lane isn't turning."

Infuriated, I floored the gas pedal, whipped the car into oncoming traffic, pulled ahead of the other cars, and into the turn lane right behind the person blocking traffic.

"Are you insane?" Lisa asked. "You're going to kill us! It's a baptism service. We'll get there when we get there."

"Well, we'd be fine if it wasn't for this moron in front of us blocking the entire intersection!"

I shoved the palm of my hand on the horn and sat back in my seat. The driver looked into his rearview mirror, unable to hear what I was saying, but clearly able to see my mouth moving, my arms waving around like a madman, and the angry expression on my face.

"I'm going to be late because of this idiot."

I slammed the horn again, this time holding it for at least ten seconds.

Then Lisa leaned over and asked, "Hey, isn't that the guy you introduced me to as we were heading out of church today?"

MISGUIDING CHRISTIANS

One of the most frightening passages in the Bible is 1 Timothy 4:16: "Watch your life and doctrine closely. Persevere in them, because if you do, you will save both yourself and your hearers."

What scares me about the verse is the implication: We can be responsible for other people going to hell by how we live *and* by what we teach.

MISGUIDING LIFESTYLES

Most Christians intuitively understand that the way we live can turn people away from Christianity. In fact, there may have been a time when you yourself turned away from Jesus because of a less than committed Christian. The apostle Peter tried to counteract this among first-century believers by advising them to be a godly example: "Live such good lives among the pagans that, though they accuse you of doing wrong, they may see your good deeds and glorify God on the day he visits us" (1 Peter 2:12).

Living a godly life among non-Christians is pretty simple to do:

Be kind.

Don't gossip at work.

Be the kind of neighbor your neighbors would want to have.

Don't blow past jittery first-time church visitors like some NASCAR driver on crack, *especially if you're the pastor*.

Generally, it's an easy principle to put into practice.

MISGUIDING BELIEFS

What's not as readily understood or obeyed among Christians is the "what we teach" part. Our words can be responsible for propelling another person headlong toward the gates of hell. It's one thing not to share the gospel with someone. That's an error of omission. But potentially misdirecting someone through wrong teaching, possibly for all eternity—that's a heavy responsibility to lay on someone, especially for those who are still brand-new Christians trying to figure out this whole Christianity thing for themselves.

But it's true. As Christians, not only can we save ourselves and our hearers by what we teach, we can damn ourselves and our hearers as well.

But there's something even worse than that.

Christians can negatively impact what another Christian believes. We can influence another Christian to stop believing in hell. The end result of that action is much worse than directing one non-Christian to hell. When one Christian influences another to stop believing in hell, it has ripple effects throughout that person's life. As John Mott wrote, "The greatest hindrances to the evangelization of the world are those *within* the church."[2]

If you rob a Christian of apocalyptic urgency, you lose every single non-Christian that person could have reached in his or her lifetime. Instead of becoming a Christian who multiplies thirty, sixty, or a hundred times, like Jesus talked about in the parable of the sower (Matt. 13:23), this person will become a believer whose influence is metaphorically buried in the ground.

HIGH-PROFILE TRAIN WRECK

On June 20, 2005, Larry King interviewed *New York Times* best-selling author and celebrity TV evangelist Joel Osteen. Halfway through the interview, King began grilling Osteen on his Christian beliefs, eventually touching on whether or not Osteen thought non-Christians would go to heaven. Here are a few key excerpts from that exchange:

> King: What if you're Jewish or Muslim, you don't accept Christ at all?
>
> Osteen: You know, I'm very careful about saying who would and wouldn't go to heaven. I don't know …
>
> King: If you believe you have to believe in Christ? They're wrong, aren't they?

> Osteen: Well, I don't know if I believe they're wrong.... But I just think that only God [will] judge a person's heart.

Later in the program, a Christian woman called in to follow up on this exchange. Osteen's response was telling:

> Caller: ....I'm wondering, though, why you sidestepped Larry's earlier question about how we get to heaven? The bible clearly tells us that Jesus is the way, the truth and the light and the only way to the father is through him [sic]....
>
> Osteen: Yes, I would agree with her. I believe that ...
>
> King: So then a Jew is not going to heaven?
>
> Osteen: No. Here's my thing, Larry, is I can't judge somebody's heart....
>
> King: But you believe your way.
>
> Osteen: I believe my way. I believe my way with all my heart.
>
> King: But for someone who doesn't share it is wrong, isn't he?

> Osteen: Well, yes. Well, I don't know if I look at it like that. I would present my way, but I'm just going to let [God] be the judge of that. I don't know. I don't know....
>
> King: What about atheists?
>
> Osteen: You know what ... I'm going to let [God] be the judge of who goes to heaven and hell. I just—again, I present the truth, and I say it every week. You know, I believe it's a relationship with Jesus. But you know what? I'm not going to go around telling everybody else if they don't want to believe that that's going to be their choice.... God's got to look at your heart, and only [God] knows that.[3]

Really?

The most recognized pastor in America has an opportunity to go on national television and share the gospel with millions of people, and keeps repeating *I don't know?* Can you imagine the apostle Paul talking like that?

Osteen's words remind me of H. Richard Niebuhr's comment about the liberal theologians of his day who preached that "a God without wrath brought men without sin into a Kingdom without judgment through the ministrations of a Christ without a Cross."[4]

What frightens me aren't all the non-Christians who heard Osteen. That's scary enough when you think about it. But imagine the impact his words had on all the Christians watching that night. What Christians needed to hear that night was certainty.

Certainty about what the Bible teaches.

Certainty about what Osteen believes the Bible teaches.

Christians need to know that it's more important for a Christian to lovingly defend the truth of the Bible than to look like a tolerant person.

Unfortunately, that didn't happen.

TELLING THE TRUTH

Contrary to what anyone might tell you, there is no ambiguity whatsoever regarding what happens to a person who dies without giving his or her life to Christ. Second Thessalonians shows us how the apostle Paul would have answered Larry King.

> God is just: He will pay back trouble to those who trouble you and give relief to you who are troubled, and to us as well. This will happen when the Lord Jesus is revealed from heaven in blazing fire with his powerful angels. He will punish those who do not know God and do not obey the gospel of our Lord Jesus. They will be punished with everlasting destruction and shut out from the presence of the Lord and from the glory of his might. (2 Thess. 1:6–9)

Let me highlight a few key phrases to help you fully grasp what Paul is saying.

"God Is Just"

Our spiritually tolerant culture has indoctrinated us to believe that "God is a loving God." While it is true that God is love, He is equally a God of justice.

"He Will Punish"

Because God is a God of justice, He is just as concerned with inflicting judgment upon His creation when it sins as He is with loving it. This is absolutely counter to what many Christians believe, but this is what the Bible plainly teaches (more about that later).

"Those Who Don't Know God or Obey the Gospel of Our Lord Jesus"

Who will this just God punish? It's very clear: those who have offended His holy nature by their sin and failed to respond to His gracious offer of forgiveness through His Son, Jesus. Current estimates put the worldwide population at roughly seven billion people. Since a little more than two billion people claim to adhere to the Christian faith, this leaves five billion people alive today who are headed toward punishment.

"Punished with Everlasting Destruction"

How will this God punish these five billion people if they don't become Christians before they die? They won't be annihilated. They won't pay for their sins in purgatory, as many Christians believe, and then be released to join everyone else in heaven. God will punish them with eternal pain, hopelessness, meaningless, and despair. As one New Testament scholar translates this verse, "They will pay the penalty of eternal ruin."[5]

"Shut Out from the Presence of the Lord"

Finally, the worst part about this tragedy is that God will withdraw from those being punished—they will not feel His presence. After death all non-Christians will exist in a place where everything that God is—hope, love, goodness, joy, etc.—is completely absent.

Here's the crux of our entire existence: If this is what the Bible teaches, then it's the obligation of every Christian (not just pastors) to boldly share the truth. If you weren't a Christian, wouldn't you want a Christian to lovingly share this with you? Can you imagine what a non-Christian would say if they had watched Joel Osteen's interview that day, died the next morning, and faced a Christ-less eternity?

There's no ambiguity about this topic. I bring this up not to denigrate Joel Osteen, because despite this very public theological fiasco, I'm sure he's doing some good things through his ministry. I bring this up as a wake-up call for all of us. Everyday Christians have an opportunity to influence not three million viewers but two or three non-Christians—over a working lunch, or while standing in line for a concert, or during a Bible study. If we fail to present the biblical facts about a non-Christian's spiritual status before God, we have failed in our most basic duty as Christ followers.

The apostle Paul's warning in 2 Timothy 4:1–5 stands as a sober reminder that there will always be some Christians who are afraid to tell the truth.

> In the presence of God and of Christ Jesus, who will judge the living and the dead, and in view of his appearing and his kingdom, I give you this charge:

> Preach the word; be prepared in season and out of season; correct, rebuke and encourage—with great patience and careful instruction. For the time will come when people will not put up with sound doctrine. Instead, to suit their own desires, they will gather around them a great number of teachers to say what their itching ears want to hear. They will turn their ears away from the truth and turn aside to myths. But you, keep your head in all situations, endure hardship, do the work of an evangelist, discharge all the duties of your ministry.

If there ever was a time that passage needed to be understood, felt, and obeyed, it's today.

FALSE TEACHERS

While Jesus was alive, He warned His disciples, "Many false prophets will appear and deceive many people" (Matt. 24:11).

Very shortly after His resurrection and the birth of the early church, His words became a reality. False teachers sprang up everywhere. As the early church evangelized people all over the Mediterranean world, new converts began to deviate from orthodox Christian teaching.

In fact, the presence of false teachers became so great that Jesus' own brother, a man named Jude, felt the need to write a letter to all the known churches at the time. The book of Jude, as it's called in the New Testament, is actually an ancient version of those forwarded emails that my mom sends me sixteen times a week. "This is really important" she'll type at the top of an email. Then I'll have to scroll down six pages just to find the original email.

Jude's letter was like the forwarded email of the early church. Scholars call it a "General Epistle," meaning it was addressed to all Christians everywhere. Copied and sent off to church after church, the letter began:

> Dear friends, although I was very eager to write to you about the salvation we share, I felt compelled to write and urge you to contend for the faith that was once for all entrusted to God's holy people. For certain individuals whose condemnation was written about long ago have secretly slipped in among you. (Jude vv. 3–4)

Other apostles and church leaders sent similar warnings to churches they helped oversee:

> There will be false teachers among you. They will secretly introduce destructive heresies. (2 Peter 2:1)

> Do not be carried away by all kinds of strange teachings. (Heb. 13:9)

> See that what you have heard from the beginning remains in you. If it does, you also will remain in the Son and in the Father. (1 John 2:24)

The adjectives the apostles used to describe false teachers are ruthless:

> Cunning, crafty, and deceitful schemers (Eph. 4:14); Conceited and understanding nothing (1 Tim. 6:3–5); Detestable, disobedient, and unfit for doing anything good (v. 10); Rebellious, mere talkers, and deceivers (Titus 1:10); Grumblers, faultfinders, and flatterers (Jude 1:16); Exploiters (2 Peter 2:3); and seducers (v. 14)

While those adjectives may seem harsh, I can tell you from personal experience they're both accurate and well deserved.

MY EXPERIENCE

Of all the places where the core aspects of my faith should have been strengthened, I would have expected it to be seminary. Instead, the exact opposite happened—the core aspects of my faith were systematically obliterated, and by fellow Christians, too. When recalling his early educational experiences, C. S. Lewis described one of his teachers as someone who "little by little, unconsciously, unintentionally … loosened the whole framework, blunted all the sharp edges, of my belief."[6]

Yet there was nothing unconscious or unintentional about what one of my seminary professors did. Every Monday, Wednesday, and Friday from 1:00 p.m. to 2:30 p.m. in the fall semester of my second year, this teacher took a pickax to the foundation of my evangelical beliefs. I had a standing appointment three times a week for theological demolition. The problem was, as with many atheists and agnostics, this professor intended only to destroy the foundation; he had no intention of replacing it with anything.

Jesus warned, "Watch out for false prophets. They come to you in sheep's clothing, but inwardly they are ferocious wolves" (Matt. 7:15). I never really understood the meaning of that passage until I fell under that professor's influence.

Little by little, as I sat under his teaching, I found myself questioning everything—whether or not I could believe in a loving God; the existence of eternal punishment for non-Christians; whether or not I could trust anything in the Bible; whether or not I made a huge mistake by signing on to become a pastor and investing years of my life in school to prepare to be one.

Eventually my struggle became so great that I started to lose sleep. I began having panic attacks. I grew depressed. I kept asking myself, *Why would Jesus have to die on the cross if everyone goes to heaven when they die? It makes no sense. And if Jesus didn't have to die, what else isn't true about Christianity?*

I realized I was in trouble, so I went to this professor's office seeking counsel.

"I don't know if I can believe in hell anymore," I said.

"Tell me more," he replied.

"I mean, isn't it just ridiculous to think that billions of people follow God to the best of their ability within the structures of their own religions, and just because they don't accept our version of God they're going to go to hell?"

"Yep. Pretty ridiculous if you ask me," he said. "Pretty judgmental if you ask me."

"And besides, like you've been saying in class, we can't trust anything that's taught in the Bible. Those people were just children of their own time periods."

"Go on."

"And miracles? Like you've been teaching, there are miracle stories in other pagan religions that Christians probably copied when they invented the stories of Jesus later put in the Gospels, and what if they were making up the whole resurrection thing as well? Paul says if there's no resurrection, there's no Christian hope, right? I don't know what I believe anymore."

"Well, Brian, we've never talked about this, but let me come clean with you. I can say this because we're one-on-one, outside of class. *I don't believe in any of that*—the inspiration of Scripture, hell, the resurrection of Jesus, miracles—*none of it.*"

"None of it?"

"Not a bit."

"What happened?"

"For years I struggled with the same questions you're wrestling with, and all I can say is that I decided I had to be honest with myself. One night as I was lying in bed, I looked up at the ceiling and said, 'I don't believe any of this anymore,' and went to sleep.

"And do you want to guess what happened?"

"What?"

"I got up the next morning and the world didn't end. The sun came out, children were playing outside, and birds chirped outside my window.

"Brian, follow your gut on this. The world won't end. The universe will be okay without Christians running around trying to convert everybody."

And do you know what I did?

I went home that night, and right before I fell asleep, I looked up at the ceiling and said, "I don't believe this anymore."

And do you want to guess what happened?

You're probably thinking that I got up the next morning and the world didn't end. The sun came out, children were playing outside, and birds chirped outside my window.

It would have been very poetic.

Instead, when I got up the next morning it was raining outside; I accidentally stepped in poop from our new puppy, and I had a killer migraine from not getting any sleep the night before.

As for "the universe will be okay" part of his counsel, that was a crock too. I was miserable. It took me six months to believe in God again, and then a number of years before I believed in hell again.

That's a long time to live without apocalyptic urgency.

All because of one "Christian."

EVERYDAY FALSE TEACHERS

Here's the danger—when I read New Testament warnings about false teachers, my mind conjures up images of the bearded, Birkenstock sandal-wearing, pipe-smoking seminary professor who destroyed my faith. He never should have set foot inside a Christian seminary. If only false teachers were that easy to recognize.

The reality is that the types of false teachers the apostles confronted had very little in common with my seminary professor. They were everyday people with regular jobs who were trying to raise families and do their best to make life work. They were normal people who had their own ideas of how Christianity ought to be taught, and freely expressed those ideas over dinner, on the job, or while caring for their children.

The cunning, crafty, and deceitful false teachers the apostles mention were twenty-six-year-old moms with two kids, farmers down the road, and the fisherman everyone rubbed shoulders with at the market. Occasionally it was the pastor who went off the deep end, but more often than not it was the everyday soccer mom on the street that everybody knew.

The stark reality is that you and I can become false teachers at any time.

Or we can be influenced by one.

That's why the biblical advice for how to interact with false teachers is just as stern as the words used to describe them:

> Command certain people not to teach false doctrines any longer. (1 Tim. 1:3)
>
> Guard what has been entrusted to your care. (6:20)
>
> Defend the gospel. (see Phil. 1:16)
>
> Refute those who oppose it. (Titus 1:9)
>
> Stand firm. (2 Thess. 2:15)
>
> Fight the battle well. (1 Tim. 1:18)

Admittedly, those are all hard things to do when the person who's teaching false doctrine is your grandmother, your friend in accounting, or your small-group leader. Yet these are some of the important but unpleasant duties of every Christian.

EVERYONE IS ACCOUNTABLE

Outside of Billy Graham, there was probably no more influential twentieth-century Christian than Mother Teresa. When asked if people became Christians before they died through her ministry to the poor in Calcutta, Mother Teresa responded,

> Oh, I hope I am converting. I don't mean what you think.... If in coming face to face with God we accept Him in our lives, then we are converting. We become a better Hindu, a better Muslim, a better Catholic, a better whatever we are, and then by being better we come closer and closer to Him. If we accept Him fully in our lives, then that is conversion. What approach would I use? For me, naturally, it would be a Catholic one, for you it may be Hindu, for someone else, Buddhist, according to each one's conscience.[7]

How do you think the apostle Paul would have responded if he overheard Mother Teresa make that statement?

He would have rebuked her! No question about it.

"No way," some might say. "This is Mother Teresa, a selfless saint who dedicated herself to serve the poor and destitute. I could see Paul going nuts on Joel Osteen but not Mother Teresa!"

I wouldn't be so sure.

We are talking, after all, about the same Paul who opposed the apostle Peter "to his face" (Gal. 2:11), and rebuked him in front of his entire congregation in Antioch (v. 14) for inaccuracy in his teaching.

Jesus Himself clearly taught, "I am the way and the truth and the life. No one comes to the Father except through me" (John 14:6). Did Mother Teresa get a memo from heaven stating that Jesus changed His mind?

The apostle Paul warned, "If we or an angel from heaven should preach a gospel other than the one we preached to you, let them be under God's curse! As we have already said, so now I say again: If anybody is preaching to you a gospel other than what you accepted, let them be under God's curse!" (Gal. 1:8–9).

That includes seminary professors.

And soccer moms.

Your mechanic.

Your Sunday-school teacher.

Your grandmother.

Even me.

And you.

And Joel Osteen.

And believe it or not, even Mother Teresa.

NOTES

1. Martin Luther, *Commentary on the Epistle to the Galatians,* trans. Theodore Graebner (Whitefish, MT: Kessinger Publishing, 2004), 26.

2. John R. Mott, *The Evangelization of the World in This Generation* (New York: Student Volunteer Movement, 1905), 49.

3. "Interview with Joel Osteen," *Larry King Live,* June 20, 2005, http://transcripts.cnn.com/TRANSCRIPTS/0506/20/lkl.01.html.

4. H. Richard Niebuhr, *Kingdom of God in America* (Chicago: Willet, Clark and Company, 1937), 193.

5. Abraham J. Malherbe, *The Letters to the Thessalonians* (New Haven, CT: Yale University Press, 2004), 401.

6. C. S. Lewis, *Surprised by Joy* (New York: Harcourt, 1955), 60.

7. Mother Teresa, *Daily Readings with Mother Teresa*, ed. Teresa de Bertodano (London: HarperCollins, 1994), 74.

5

SIDETRACKED

> If you read history you will find that the Christians who did most for the present world were just those who thought most of the next.... Aim at Heaven and you will get earth 'thrown in': aim at earth and you will get neither.
>
> —*C. S. Lewis*[1]

When I saw her teeth, I wanted to kick the chairs over in the room. I've never felt so helpless and enraged at the same time.

"Her teeth," I said to my wife, Lisa, under my breath. "They're black. How did this happen? I feel like I'm going to go nuts—on someone, something, I don't care. This is unacceptable."

Virginiah speaks Swahili, so she didn't understand what I was saying.

"And this is a coloring book," Lisa said to Virginiah as she pulled it out of the bag of gifts we had brought for her to open. "You can color it with these crayons."

As Lisa kept pulling items from the bag, such as underwear, sunglasses, a toothbrush, stickers, and a stream of other gifts that any six-year-old girl would love, especially one from the slums of Nairobi, all Virginiah kept saying was, "Wow."

Our family began sponsoring Virginiah two years prior to meeting her. She lives in the slums of Nairobi, Kenya, in an area called the Mathare Valley, home to eight hundred thousand people who live in tiny steel shanties and make an average of less than one dollar a day. Things look bleak for a little girl like Virginiah. It's estimated that 80 percent of the women here work in the sex trade. Until we came into her life, she was headed for a hopeless future. Our sponsorship gives Virginiah two meals a day, an education, medical care, the watchful care of a social worker, and the loving support of local pastors and church leaders.[2]

On this particular trip, we came with a group of twenty-one people from our church to host a week-long medical clinic. Every day lines of anxious patients wrapped around the building, hoping for the chance to be seen. While the clinic saw patients outside, Lisa conducted administrator training for the head teachers of the ten schools our church helps to sponsor. I trained the pastors of our partnering churches in evangelism and church growth. In between our commitments that week, we met Virginiah for the first time.

As we sat in a classroom along with nineteen other people from our church, waiting for the social workers to bring in the children we all sponsored, I couldn't remember the last time I felt so nervous.

At first we weren't sure whether or not we'd actually meet Virginiah. Our church's mission trip coincided with the 2010 national referendum vote in Kenya. Two years prior, violence broke out in the slums during the national elections. Most people assumed history would repeat itself, so parents sent their children into the rural countryside to stay with relatives. Social workers had to comb the slums for hours looking for Virginiah, but they finally found her. She was the last child to enter the room.

Lisa walked over, picked her up, gave her a huge hug, and sat her down on her lap. I leaned over and kissed her on the forehead. Virginiah immediately recognized us from the pictures and letters we had sent. A little intimidated by all the white Americans in the room snapping pictures, Virginiah spoke very softly. Her teacher sat next to us and translated our English into Swahili and back.

I have to say that our encounter could have been one of the most spiritually intense feel-good moments of my life, but one thing prevented that: I couldn't stop staring at her teeth.

They were black.

And rotted.

After twenty minutes, we gave each other hugs and took a few final pictures. Then Lisa walked Virginiah back out to her aunt and brother, and I went hunting for the director of the mission.

"I'm sure I'm not the first person to ask this question," I said to my friend Keith Ham. "But how do we take her home with us?"

"Who?"

"Virginiah."

Stepping back and taking a deep breath, he said, "Listen, we're here to empower the families, and you're doing a good thing. Even though she's an orphan, her aunt is taking care of her. She already has a loving family. You're changing that kid's life."

"But did you see her teeth? They're rotted and black. What happened?"

"Malnutrition and poor hygiene. She was that way before she ever came to us."

"All because she didn't have enough food and a toothbrush?"

"Yep."

"Keith, I don't care what it costs; she's got to see a dentist. Like right now."

"There's one coming in from a church in California next week. I'll have him look at her."

"Whatever it costs."

"Okay."

"I'm serious. I mean it, Keith."

"*Okay*."

HOLY RAGE

People always say that the loving people among us make the biggest difference in the lives of hurting and broken people. *I beg to differ*. I think the angriest people make the biggest difference. Look through the pages of history and you'll quickly discover that those filled with holy rage against the dehumanizing effects of slavery, malnutrition, preventable diseases, and the like have made the greatest contribution to humanity. Something within them rose up and motivated them to shout, "I've had enough! I'm going to do something to change this."

The Bible tells us that at the end of the ages, Jesus will stand before His followers and say, "Come, you who are blessed by my Father; take your inheritance, the kingdom prepared for you since the creation of the world. For I was hungry and you gave me something to eat, I was thirsty and you gave me something to drink, I was a stranger and you invited me in, I needed clothes and you clothed me, I was sick and you looked after me, I was in prison and you came to visit me" (Matt. 25:34–36).

Whenever I used to read that passage, I pictured Jesus addressing a room jam-packed with old, diminutive nuns walking around with hands folded, lovingly singing Gregorian chants. While I'm sure there will be lots of nuns standing before Jesus on that day—I've known a number who have given their lives away for the cross—I now believe that most of the people Jesus will address will be ordinary folks with anger issues. Like the fifty-six-year-old businessman I know who got so sick of kids not having clean drinking water that he started a company to solve the problem. Or the thirty-year-old mom who started collecting shoes for the homeless and now has quite literally become the feet of Jesus to thousands in need. Or the forty-three-year-old woman who started a ministry that is helping hundreds of prostitutes find new beginnings.

It all started with holy rage.

Our church has gotten angry too.

In ten years' time, the people of our church will have given over 1.5 million dollars to rescue kids from the hopelessness of the Nairobi slums. And if there's anything we can possibly do to raise more, we'll try to double that number. Like many of our partners, our church has been seized by the conviction that no kid should grow up with rotten teeth.

Or fear walking outside her shanty and being gang raped.

Or have a prostitute for a mom.

Or have a dad who sniffs glue.

Or be unable to read.

Or have a baby at age thirteen.

Or die of AIDS at age fifteen.

What are the things that make you angry about the world we live in that you'd like to change?

WHAT A DIFFERENCE A MILLENNIUM MAKES

It's exciting to watch God give the twenty-first century church a holy rage and a desire to right the rampant injustices in our world. When I look back upon my days in my high school youth group, I remember a lot of sleepovers and putt-putt outings. In contrast, my daughters are constantly talking about the need for our church to help stop human trafficking. Social justice, formerly a series of issues championed by mainline liberal denominations in America, is now a front-burner issue for almost all evangelical Christians. Thank God for that.

In many ways the evangelical community is simply following what world leaders have set as a priority. On September 8, 2000, following a three-day summit at the headquarters of the United Nations, 147 heads of state signed what became known as the *Millennium Declaration*, a bold manifesto laying out eight goals to be achieved by 2015. Together these countries pledged to combine their resources to jointly eradicate a significant percentage of extreme poverty, hunger, illiteracy, and disease around the world. Along with these goals they also established targets for achieving gender equality and the empowerment of women, environmental sustainability, and a global partnership for development. Here are just a few of the targets they're working toward:

Goal 1: Eradicate extreme poverty and hunger

- Halve, between 1990 and 2015, the proportion of people whose income is less than $1 a day

Goal 2: Achieve universal primary education

- Ensure that, by 2015, children everywhere, boys

and girls alike, will be able to complete a full course of primary schooling

Goal 3: Promote gender equality and empower women

- Eliminate gender disparity in primary and secondary education, preferably by 2005, and in all levels of education no later than 2015

Goal 4: Reduce child mortality

- Reduce by two thirds, between 1990 and 2015, the under-five mortality rate

Goal 5: Improve maternal health

- Reduce by three-quarters, between 1990 and 2015, the maternal mortality ratio
- Achieve, by 2015, universal access to reproductive health

Goal 6: Combat HIV/AIDS, malaria, and other diseases

- Have halted by 2015 and begun to reverse the spread of HIV/AIDS

Goal 7: Ensure environmental sustainability

- Integrate the principles of sustainable development into country policies and programmes and reverse the loss of environmental resources

Goal 8: Develop a global partnership for development

- Develop further an open, rule-based, predictable, non-discriminatory trading and financial system[3]

I love that list.

I'm inspired by that list.

As a Christian, I would love nothing more than to see every single goal on the list met by the year 2015. These priorities are no different from the causes Christians throughout the ages have championed—feed the hungry, minister to the sick, and serve those who have no voice.

Yet, if that list is meant to be an all-encompassing manifesto for the change we need throughout our world, there's one little goal missing. The world leaders from 147 countries around the world forgot to add goal number 9:

Goal 9: Evangelize the world

- Help Christians throughout the world recapture apocalyptic urgency
- Work together to help seven billion human beings avoid the full brunt of God's wrath in hell after they die

I believe that Jesus would say that if Christians throw their hats into the ring with the world to accomplish the first eight goals but don't accomplish the ninth, our zeal to fix the world's problems will inadvertently create the single greatest holocaust human civilization has ever seen. As wonderful as it is to educate illiterate children or reduce biodiversity loss in developing countries, none of the goals in the *Millennium Declaration* are more important than the goal I added.

In the first two chapters we looked at two reasons why Christians lose apocalyptic urgency. In chapter three we explored how we allow non-Christians to make us feel stupid for believing in hell. And in chapter four we investigated how we allow other Christians to deceive us into thinking hell doesn't really exist. Before we move on to the next chapter and explore what creates apocalyptic urgency in our hearts, it's important to address one final reason people lose that urgency to reach their friends and family for Christ.

Christians lose apocalyptic urgency when they become preoccupied with important kingdom-related activities like feeding the poor and fighting for human rights. Over time they allow these activities to take precedence over helping people get to heaven. They let their passion and God-inspired holy rage for certain causes reshape their understanding of God's priorities and His plan for our world.

This happens for a few easily understandable reasons.

First, when Christians show kindness to the poor, non-Christians don't make fun of us. When was the last time an atheist made fun of you for giving food to the needy? It just doesn't happen. Non-Christians assume this is the kind of activity Christians should undertake. In fact, non-Christians ridicule Christians when they're *not* involved in social justice issues.

Second, there's immediate personal gratification involved in this kind of work. You help someone get off the streets and it immediately becomes one of those "*Extreme Makeover: Home Edition*" moments that tugs on your heartstrings and causes everyone around you to pat you on the back and well up with tears. Contrast that with the awkwardness you feel when you even remotely suggest to your Hindu coworker that her beliefs may be incorrect.

So I understand why Christians focus on meeting social needs rather than trying to help their non-Christian family members and friends become Christians.

But just because something is understandable doesn't mean it's right.

SIDETRACKED CHRISTIANS

In August of 2005 our church planned an offering appeal to plant new churches throughout the New York City area. We planned our appeal to occur on September 11, 2005, the four-year anniversary of the 9/11 terrorist attacks. Since we are a church-planting church and New York City is one of the largest mission fields in the United States, we anticipated a large offering. We sent letters with envelopes to the congregation ahead of time. We showed special videos in our services to highlight the need. We expected and hoped for a miraculous move of God in people's hearts on that day.

Then Katrina hit.

When Hurricane Katrina formed offshore on August 23, 2005, ripped through the Gulf Coast region, and finally dissipated on August 30, 2005, it left the single-greatest natural disaster our country had ever experienced in its wake. Like all Christians at the time, we knew we had to respond. September 4 was Labor Day weekend, and we knew that a large percentage of our congregation would be gone, so we waited until September 11 to make a church-wide appeal.

The only problem was that we already had one offering planned for that day.

After a lot of prayer, our leadership team decided to do something we had never done before—we would take up two large offerings on the same day: one for New York City evangelism, and the other for Katrina relief. So on Sunday, September 11, 2005, nineteen days after Katrina hit, we took up two offerings.

I stood up before the church and said,

> Our church has never made two offering appeals at once. I know we are not an overly wealthy congregation, so I'm sure some of you are conflicted about where to send your money. It's my prayer that you will be generous to both. However, if you have to choose, give your money to help start new churches in New York City to reach people who aren't Christians yet. What good would it be if we gave money to help people who are already Christians rebuild a home, a temporary need, and didn't give money to help reach people who are going to hell? Trust me, if someone in New Orleans was truly a Christian and understood what their faith was all about, they would stand up here and tell you they'd rather be homeless before they stood in the way of someone going to heaven.

A man in the back of the auditorium immediately stood up and made a huge commotion, then pointed his finger and screamed at me for saying something he considered so reckless and hateful. He kicked chairs on the way out. A few people followed him. I thought I was going to have an all-out mutiny on my hands.

Since that day I've had a lot of time to think about how my words sounded to some of the people in attendance. I've thought about my words long and hard, and if I had to say it all over again, I would have said it exactly the same way. I wouldn't have changed one word.

Let me share three reasons why.

WHY EVANGELISM TAKES PRECEDENCE OVER SOCIAL JUSTICE

1. Scripture, Not Human Compassion, Guides a Disciple's Priorities

You can be the most compassionate person in the world and spend your entire life helping those in need, but if you don't submit the totality of your life, efforts, and teaching to the *totality* of what is taught in the Bible, you have committed a grave mistake. The same Jesus who taught, "When you give to the needy" (Matt. 6:2) also taught, "Go and make disciples of all nations" (28:19).

There aren't two versions of Christianity that Christ followers get to choose from—the one modeled by the compassionate Jesus, and the other modeled by the "go forth and spread the gospel" Jesus. *They're the same Jesus.* At the last day all believers will be held accountable for both requirements. The Bible says in 2 Timothy 3:16, "All Scripture is God-breathed." All of it—not just the parts we like, but every single command. Every teaching of Jesus applies to every single Christian, at all times, in all locations, without exception.

When my grandmother moved into the Cardinal Village Retirement Center in Columbus, Ohio, she became very good friends with a woman named Helen, who lived directly across the hall. Once, when my family visited her, she asked everyone if they would like some freshly made chocolate chip cookies. My dad, knowing that her pantry was empty (he shopped for her) asked, "Where did you get the ingredients for those cookies?"

Grandma said, "Helen across the hall made them for me. She knows I have a sweet tooth, so we worked out an arrangement. Every time I give her one of my Darvocet pills (a very strong narcotic painkiller), she'll bake me a dozen chocolate chip cookies."

"What!" everyone shouted.

"Yes," she said. "We've been doing this for a while now!"

"Grandma, you can't do that," my sister Laura said. "That's illegal. You've become Helen's drug dealer!"

"But she's in *so* much pain!"

Now I'm not suggesting that you should be on the most-wanted list of the Bureau of Alcohol, Tobacco, Firearms and Explosives the way my seventy-six–year-old grandma should have been, but if you're content with simply meeting physical needs, without helping people find God, you're just as misguided.

Never forget that the Bible alone should dictate our priorities as Christ followers, not human compassion. Compassion without truth will make a person do very kind (but stupid) things. What else would you call the act of helping somebody find their daily bread but never helping them discover the "bread of life" (John 6:35)?

2. Jesus Didn't Need to Die for God's People to Care for the Poor

I have a pastor friend who doesn't believe in hell. Whenever the topic comes up, I always ask him a simple question for which he has no answer: "If everyone goes to heaven after they die, and the point of Christianity is to do good on the earth, then why did Jesus have to die on the cross?"

He's never provided an answer.

Because there isn't one.

What Christians must realize is that the old covenant had wonderful provisions to care for the poor and the oppressed. Jesus didn't have to come to earth and die to make the world a better place. God's people, the Jewish nation, already did that.

Concern for the poor was a distinctive feature of Jewish law and tradition:

> Do not go over your vineyard a second time or pick up the grapes that have fallen. Leave them for the poor and the foreigner. I am the LORD your God. (Lev. 19:10)

> If anyone is poor among your fellow Israelites in any of the towns of the land the LORD your God is giving you, do not be hardhearted or tightfisted toward them. Rather, be openhanded and freely lend them whatever they need.… There will always

> be poor people in the land. Therefore I command you to be openhanded toward your fellow Israelites who are poor and needy in your land. (Deut. 15:7–8, 11)

> For six years you are to sow your fields and harvest the crops, but during the seventh year let the land lie unplowed and unused. Then the poor among your people may get food from it, and the wild animals may eat what is left. Do the same with your vineyard and your olive grove. (Ex. 23:10–11)

The Old Testament prophets championed the rights of the poor and oppressed.

> "He defended the cause of the poor and needy, and so all went well. Is that not what it means to know me?" declares the LORD. (Jer. 22:16)

God's heart has always beaten fast for the orphans and widows. I believe in what theologians call "God's preferential option for the poor." I believe that all of God's people, at all times, and in every way, should reduce their lifestyle so they can become Jesus' arms to wrap around a needy and hurting world. But let's be very clear about one thing: Jesus died on the cross because caring for the world wasn't enough. More burdensome than having an economic disparity problem, a health problem, or a gender inequality problem, humanity at its core has a sin problem. That's why Jesus came.

New people come to our church all the time and tell me, "We should stop trying to convert people and simply do our best to make this world a better place." I'll remind them that Christianity is a religion meant to solve a sin problem. It is not a religion meant to solve all the problems of this world. It is not a system of religious thought meant to usher in Utopia here on earth.

Christianity is apocalyptic. It begins with the end in mind, namely these things: This world is going to end, all humanity is racing toward final judgment, and God charged the followers of the risen Jesus with bringing the possibility of spiritual rebirth to the human race. While we are sent to carry out that mission, we also happen to love the poor, care for the downtrodden, and fight for the rights of the oppressed. We do that out of love. But followers of Jesus know that our ultimate mission is not to make this world a better place to live, as important as that is. Our mission is to give every human being on earth the news that their relationship with God can be restored through Jesus' death on the cross.

Christianity is not a "let's make the world a better place" kind of religion. It is meant to solve one issue: the problem of human sin, which has flared up the wrath of a holy God. Any attempt to make it into a religion that focuses solely on social justice falls flat and ultimately becomes ineffective. Likewise, any attempt to make Christianity into a religion devoid of social justice would be incomplete as well. It's never either/or in Scripture. But that doesn't mean evangelism isn't prioritized.

Peter Drucker, a twentieth-century leader in modern management theory, used to ask business leaders two questions to help them analyze how things were going in their workplace. First, what business are you in? Second, how's business?

What business is Christianity in? Christianity is not in the eliminate-global-warming business, as important as that is. It's not in the change-the-political-culture business. It's not in the feed-the-poor business, as absolutely crucial as that is. It's not in the stop-abortion business, as vitally important as I think that is as well. Christianity is in the wrath-deflecting business. And we need to ask ourselves, "How's business?"

3. The Early Church Prioritized Evangelism without Ignoring Social Justice

A cursory reading of the New Testament shows that the first Christians made evangelism their absolute top priority. For instance, one of the most scandalous social justice issues early church leaders could have worked to help dismantle would have been slavery. Yet no leader spoke against it. Not a word. In fact, many note that teachings like, "Slaves, obey your earthly masters with respect and fear, and with sincerity of heart" (Eph. 6:5) only seemed to perpetuate the systemic problem of slavery.

The point is the first Christians stayed focused on their main purpose: the evangelization of every single man, woman, and child on the planet. As they focused on that goal, they also worked on social justice issues, but they never veered off course. As Elton Trueblood so aptly observed, "We are surprised to see how little the early Christians dealt with current political and economical problems, if we may judge by the extant literature of that period. They did not even attack slavery, iniquitous as it must have been. They just went on building the kind of fellowship which was bound, eventually, to destroy slavery."[4]

What we have today is a situation where many who claim the name of Christ no longer feel the urgency to make evangelism their top priority. They've focused on other things. As a result, the Christian community is single-handedly helping to create the greatest tragedy this world will have ever known, all in the name of compassion. There are roughly seven billion people on this planet and best guess is that no more than two billion wear the name of Christ. That's today. That statistic doesn't take into account those who have died and those who are being born.

The early church got this issue right. Just because they used an indirect strategy to eliminate slavery doesn't mean they ignored social justice. Quite the contrary, they understood that you could focus on evangelism while not ignoring the needs of the poor and oppressed.

For example, take the story in Acts 6 in which widows were overlooked in the daily distribution of food. The way the apostles addressed the problem teaches us something about their priorities.

> So the Twelve gathered all the disciples together and said, "It would not be right for us to neglect the ministry of the word of God in order to wait on tables. Brothers and sisters, choose seven men from among you who are known to be full of the Spirit and wisdom. We will turn this responsibility over to them and will give our attention to prayer and the ministry of the word." (Acts 6:2–4)

By stopping what they were doing and fixing the problem of food distribution for the poor, the apostles affirmed the absolute importance of caring for the poor in the life and ministry of the early church. At the same time, however, the apostles made it clear which activity was the most important.

On another occasion the apostle Paul, along with Barnabas, held a strategy meeting with James, Peter, and John, the leaders of the Jerusalem church, about the focus of each of their ministries. At the end of that meeting Paul wrote,

> They agreed that we should go to the Gentiles, and they to the circumcised. All they asked was that we should continue to remember the poor, the very thing I had been eager to do all along. (Gal. 2:9–10)

It's clear that evangelism was their primary focus, but as Christ followers, they also obeyed the command to "love your neighbor as yourself" (Luke 10:27). They wanted to underscore the importance of caring for the poor. As Martin Luther observed, "Next to the preaching of the Gospel, a true and faithful pastor will take care of the poor."[5]

The apostle Paul left that meeting and stayed true to his word. As he embarked on a series of church-planting missionary journeys, he often organized offerings on behalf of the poor in Jerusalem.

> The disciples, as each one was able, decided to provide help for the brothers and sisters living in

> Judea. This they did, sending their gift to the elders by Barnabas and Saul. (Acts 11:29–30)

> After an absence of several years, I came to Jerusalem to bring my people gifts for the poor and to present offerings. (24:17)

Passages such as Romans 15:17–33, 1 Corinthians 16:3, and 2 Corinthians 8—9 make it clear that Paul's singular focus was starting new churches to reach the lost who would, in return, "proclaim good news to the poor" (Luke 4:18).

FINAL CHALLENGE

My wife is a principal, but for years taught sixth-grade science in an economically disadvantaged school district in our area. She's always had a heart for people who grew up in similar circumstances to the ones she faced.

At the end of her first day of class a few years ago, she brought home a love note one of the boys in her class had written her.

"Bet you've never written a love note to me like this one!" she said as she handed it to me in the kitchen. The next day she brought home another note just like it.

And another.

And another.

And another.

A couple weeks later she walked into the house after a long day teaching and said, "You've got some competition." Here's what the latest note said, in the boy's unedited sixth-grade grammar:

Mrs. Jones,

You are the sweetest teacher ever because your funny, famous, awsome, sweet, smart, brillint to me Mrs. Jones, and you have the beautiful brown eyes, and beautiful good smellin brown hair Mrs. Jones. Mrs. Jones you look beautiful as ever I saw you Mrs. Jones.

Mrs. Jones you smell like flowers to me Mrs. Jones because you look awsome to me today Mrs. Jones and you are fablous today Mrs. Jones.

I love you as my teacher because you are really really awsome today Mrs. Jones. Mrs. Jones you are smelling really really triple really nice today.

Mrs. Jones you are a famous awsome movie star to me Mrs. Jones.

Love Charlie

I put the note down and said, "Alright, enough is enough. Give this kid a message for me: '*One more note and I'm going to knock you out.*'"

She said, "I'm not going to do that."

I said, "Why not?"

She said, "Because he's got cancer."

There are hundreds of Charlies all around us, just waiting for someone to become the arms of Jesus that will wrap them up in His compassionate love. But as heart wrenching as these needs are, never forget that for people like Charlie, death isn't their biggest problem.

Their biggest problem is dying without being prepared for death.

And that's where you and I come in.

NOTES

1. C. S. Lewis, *Mere Christianity* (New York: HarperCollins, 1980), 134.

2. For more information go to http://cmfi.org/partner/hopepartnership.

3. "The Millenium Development Goals Report," United Nations Department of Economic and Social Affairs (2009), http://www.un.org/millenniumgoals/pdf/MDG_Report_2009_ENG.pdf.

4. Elton Trueblood, *Alternative to Futility* (New York: Harper & Brothers, 1948), 31–32.

5. Martin Luther, *Commentary on the Epistle to the Galatians,* trans. Theodore Graebner (Whitefish, MT: Kessinger Publishing, 2004), 43.

PART THREE

IF HELL IS REAL ... HOW CAN I GET SERIOUS ABOUT IT?

6
WRATH

When one preaches Christianity in such a way that the echo answers,
"Away with that man from the earth, he does not deserve to live,"
know then that this is the Christianity of the New Testament … capital
punishment is the penalty for preaching Christianity as it truly is.

—*Søren Kierkegaard*[1]

When I was in third grade, I took a flare, the kind used by police to direct traffic after an accident, and plunged its red-hot burning flame into a container full of gasoline. To this day I still cringe whenever I think about that moment. The fact that I'm alive to tell you about it is, I believe, a result of God's miraculous intervention.

It happened in the late spring of 1979, a few weeks before school let out for the summer, and for reasons I still don't fully understand, my friend Chris and I thought it would be fun to take a box of matches from his parents' kitchen and start lighting things on fire in his backyard. Now, let me pause and acknowledge the obvious elephant in the room: You've probably seen enough episodes of *CSI* or *48 Hours Mystery* to know how virtually all criminals in federal prisons went bad when they started playing with matches, so I understand if you want to begin psychoanalyzing me.

However, I also need to point out that there are just as many studies out there pointing to links between neurotic ax-murdering tendencies and people who buy and read Christian books. So before you get yourself all worked up playing armchair psychologist on me, let's both take a deep breath.

As I was saying, Chris and I started lighting matches and burning things. At first we just burned pieces of grass and wood chips. But that grew boring fast, so we moved on to melting the heads off plastic toy soldiers and Chris's sister's Barbies (okay, on second thought, maybe you do need to psychoanalyze me). After a while I suggested, "Let's get some gasoline from your dad's tool shed." We smiled at each other and ran to the shed with excitement. Minutes later we huddled over the five-gallon lawnmower gasoline container, dipped things into it, and watched them ignite.

While I was in the shed, I noticed something that looked like a stick of dynamite but knew it was a flare because I had seen my grandfather, who was a police officer, use one before. When we ran out of Barbies to melt, I turned to Chris and said, "Hey, why don't I get that flare?" I don't remember Chris's response, but I do remember walking into his dad's shed, grabbing the flare, and then ripping off the lid, which instantly ignited it. As I walked out to the backyard I held it to a worm that I had dug up and watched it squirm as I put the flame closer and closer. Within seconds it stopped wiggling and died. Chris grabbed the flare and slowly waved it over a line of green toy soldiers he had lined up. The head of each soldier instantly melted.

Then for some reason, I grabbed the flare and said, "Watch this." Inexplicably, for reasons I still do not understand, other than sheer eight-year-old naïveté (and stupidity), I shoved the flare, flame first, into the five-gallon container of gasoline.

As a parent of three children, I cringe every time I think back to this moment.

In an instant, our lives could have been forever changed.

But they weren't.

Nothing happened.

As I stood there, leaning over the container with the flare still stuck inside, Chris started backpedaling. My heart sank. Realizing the gravity of what I had just done, I quickly jerked the flare out of the container, splattering gasoline all over my shirt. Looking up, I saw Chris slowly walking backward, numb and speechless. We looked at each other, hearts racing, and eyes slowly tearing up. We didn't know exactly what just occurred, but we knew we were spared from something chilling. Overcome by a childlike fear that our parents would discover what we had done, we dragged the gasoline can back to the shed, threw the extinguished flare into the trash can, and I ran home.

I never told another person about what happened that day until I was in fifth grade. My science teacher, Mr. Will, was teaching a unit on fire, and for some reason I raised my hand and shared the story of what happened that day. When I finished the story I remember saying, "It was a miracle. That gasoline could have burned my hands."

Mr. Will lowered his eyebrows as he walked over to my desk and cleared his throat.

"Brian, I agree with you that it was a miracle. But you weren't saved from burned hands that day.

"I don't mean to scare you, but what you were really saved from was a twenty-foot high explosion that should have instantly covered you and your friend in a mushroom cloud of flames. If you were lucky, you would have died minutes later, but more than likely what would have happened is you would have suffered third-degree burns over your entire body. Your clothes would have soaked up the gasoline and you would have become a human torch, unable to stop the burning even if you wanted to. Your face would have become instantly unrecognizable: Your hair and eyebrows, gone. Your skin would have become a mixture of blood and black charred puss. Without immediate care, your internal organs would have shut down and you would have died a slow, agonizing death days later in the pediatric burn unit."

I felt like I was going to vomit. I had no idea. For two years, in my childlike limited understanding of the situation, I thought that I had simply avoided a fire; burns to the hands, maybe; possibly a grass fire that would have upset Chris's dad because he kept his lawn finely manicured. *But an explosion?* We were saved from a 530-degree-Fahrenheit cloud of flames that would have instantly melted off layers of my skin? *Permanently disfigured bodies and death?*

I had no clue.

As I sat silently in my chair, staring at the floor, Mr. Will put his hand on my shoulder and said something I'll never forget. "Brian, you have no idea what you were really saved from that day."

HALF OF THE GOSPEL

In the same way that I felt shock when I learned what should have happened to me in Chris's backyard, I believe most Christians will be shocked when they get to heaven and discover what Jesus *really* saved them from when they became Christians. The reality is that most Christians don't have a clue what happened at their conversion.

This shouldn't surprise us. Have you seen the evangelistic appeals that pastors and church leaders give to non-Christians? They sound like invitations to buy something from the *Home Shopping Network:* "Folks, for the next five minutes the opportunity to change your life is staring you right in the face. Don't wait. All you have to do is follow these easy steps and you'll be on your way to a happy, successful, and fulfilling new life in Christ."

Can you imagine the apostle Paul talking that way?

Contrary to what you might have heard when you crossed the line of faith, you weren't saved from a mediocre version of your life the day you came to Christ. You weren't baptized to escape a life of boredom. You weren't reconciled with the Creator so you could live life with meaning and purpose, free from a flabby waistline and dingy yellow teeth. Instead, Jesus rescued you from falling into the hands of Someone larger than your mind can conceive, stronger than the combined strength of a trillion nuclear explosions; a holy God destined to unleash the complete, unrestrained force of His wrath on you for offending His holy nature. That's what you were really saved from.

Apocalyptic urgency is a by-product of understanding and accepting the true nature and character of God. One of the reasons

Christians don't feel an overwhelming burden to help their friends find their way back to God is because they don't understand the nature of the God they claim to follow.

For the most part, it's not their fault. They were converted to a nice, comfy, pleasant, American Jesus. They didn't hear the entire gospel. They weren't presented the whole story. So whenever they think about the spiritual status of their non-Christian friends, helping them avoid hell is barely even on their radar. Hell wasn't a spiritual problem that drove them to become Christians to avoid it, so why would it be a problem for anyone else?

There's a saying among church planters that applies here: "What you win people with you keep them with." If someone is presented at conversion with a version of God that is cleaned up, sanitized, and neatly wrapped—a god that appeals to the masses and rivals the best self-help gurus out there—then that's the kind of god that new Christian will want to follow after his or her conversion. That new convert's expectation for his or her spiritual life will be predicated upon that original vision of who God is and what He wants to do in his or her life (which goes a long way to explain the self-sufficient, consumer-oriented nature of many American Christians).

Yes, God loves you. Yes, God wants to show you mercy and grace. Yes, Jesus died on the cross for you as an act of God's love. However, if you're not a Christian, you also need to understand that the God of the Bible thinks that your transgressions warrant execution (Rom. 1:32). He loathes your sin and considers you a personal enemy (5:10). Every single act of disobedience you commit against His will enrages Him and forces cosmic self-restraint just to keep Him from instantly obliterating you from His planet (Nah. 1:2–3).

Now some of you may already be thinking: *That's nothing new. That's all I heard growing up in church.* If that's the case, and you rarely heard a balanced presentation of God's love and God's wrath, then that church really messed with your head. We need to repair your image of God. We'll get to that in the next chapter. For now, I'd like to talk directly to those of you who are creeped out by the whole "God loathes my sin and thinks I should die" thing, which, in my experience, represents the vast majority of people.

THE WRATH OF GOD

The *wrath of God* is a phrase used in the Bible to describe God's angry response to human disobedience. The clearest expression of God's wrath is found in Romans 1:18: "The wrath of God is being revealed from heaven against all the godlessness and wickedness of people." The word for "wrath" is the Greek word *orge*, which means, "to be puffed up or become excited."[2] The Old Testament counterpart was the Hebrew word *'ap*, which has the sense of snorting.[3] Both refer to the physical transformation that takes place in someone's face when he or she is caught up in an angry explosion. However, when the biblical writers used these words, their intent wasn't to describe the transformation of God's facial features, rather the extreme brutality of his rage (e.g., plague, drought, disease, social disorder, war, exile, and death) that could be provoked at any moment by human disobedience.

The wrath of God is both a present *and* future reality. Those who have yet to become Christians are under God's wrath *right now*. Ephesians 2:3 tells us that nonbelievers are "by nature deserving of wrath." Romans 1:18 says, "The wrath of God is *being* revealed." God's wrath is a present reality, right now, right here in the twenty-first century in the lives of your friends who are far from God. But the Bible also teaches that those without Christ will experience God's wrath *in the future*. John 3:36 says, "Whoever believes in the Son has eternal life, but whoever rejects the Son will not see life, for God's wrath remains on them." As biblical scholar Douglas Moo observes, "The present experience of God's wrath is merely a foretaste of what will come on the Day of Judgment."[4]

When I think of God's wrath, I think of the day my friend's normally mild-mannered German shepherd managed to sneak into the chicken coop. The result was utter carnage—bloody feathers all over the ground, the walls, half-eaten body parts strewn about, the dog's face and body covered with blood—it was an odd sight. One minute the dog is playing with my friend's kids near the swing set, the next minute he's violently ripping apart seventeen chickens. Moments later, it's back to sitting peacefully with the kids while they're playing jump rope. I think that's what the wrath of God looks like—one moment God is calm, and the next He's provoked by human disobedience into a state of holy rage (and usually after repeated warnings).

Deuteronomy 32:40–42 gives us a glimpse of God when His fury is provoked:

> I lift my hand to heaven and solemnly swear:
> As surely as I live forever,
> when I sharpen my flashing sword
> and my hand grasps it in judgment,

I will take vengeance on my adversaries
and repay those who hate me.
I will make my arrows drunk with blood,
while my sword devours flesh:
the blood of the slain and the captives,
the heads of the enemy leaders.

If you're thinking, *Okay, that's just about as creepy as you can get,* then you're starting to gain a clearer understanding of the true character of the God in whom you've placed your trust as a Christian. In the biblical story, God's love and God's wrath are never mutually exclusive. Understandably, a vengeful deity seems like a leftover from the Dark Ages. If you think our God sounds like something you'd read about in *National Geographic,* you might understand why the second-century Roman pastor Marcion (who was viewed as a dangerous heretic) deleted the two words "of God" in Romans 1:18 in the Bibles used in the churches he served (i.e., "The wrath ~~of God~~ is being revealed from heaven").[5]

Wrath is an acceptable part of the human experience. However, the idea of the wrath *of God* is often something people struggle with, whether they live in the twenty-first century or lived in the second. Outspoken atheist Richard Dawkins wrote:

> The God of the Old Testament is arguably the most unpleasant character in all fiction: jealous and proud of it; a petty, unjust, unforgiving control-freak; a vindictive, bloodthirsty ethnic cleanser; a misogynistic, homophobic, racist, infanticidal,

> genocidal, filicidal, pestilential, megalomaniacal, sadomasochistic, capriciously malevolent bully. Those of us schooled from infancy in his ways can become desensitized to their horror.[6]

When I first read this, I was infuriated. His comments are based on two entirely false allegations.

First, the God of the Old Testament is the same God of the New Testament. In Christian theology, whatever attributes describe God in the first thirty-nine books of the Old Testament also apply to the God portrayed in the twenty-seven books of the New Testament. If the God of the Old Testament is petty, unjust, and vindictive, either the God of the New Testament bears those same characteristics, or that characterization is utterly false. There aren't two Gods in the Bible—a mean Old Testament God and a nice New Testament God—the God of Abraham, Isaac, Jacob, and Joseph is also the God of Jesus, Paul, Peter, and John.

Second, Dawkins is dead wrong, not because he paints God with too cruel of a brushstroke, but because he's too flattering. The God of the Bible is *far* more vengeful than Dawkins could ever dream. The real God, the Deity we only catch a quick glimpse of in the pages of Scripture, is infinitely more bloodthirsty, vindictive, genocidal, pestilential, sadomasochistic, and capriciously malevolent than human language could begin to express. This soft depiction does a tremendous disservice to the cause of Christ. Why? Until you realize how vengeful God really is, you'll never feel an urgency for your friends and family members who are without Christ.

WRATH IN ACTION

I'd like you to read through the following Scriptures and pay close attention to your reactions. I've taken some of Dawkins's accusations and lined them up with corresponding biblical passages. As you read them, try your best not to jump to God's defense. Place yourself in the shoes of someone who has nothing to lose by being honest about what she or he reads. Don't try to explain God's actions; instead, allow your uncensored thoughts and feelings to emerge.

"Infanticidal"

When I think of infanticide, I think of news stories: Susan Smith driving her sons into a lake, or Andrea Yates drowning her five young children in her bathtub. But praying the Lord's Prayer to a baby killer? The fact is there are many instances in Scripture where God told His leaders to kill infants. The most famous occurred in 1 Samuel 15:2–3.

> This is what the LORD Almighty says: "I will punish the Amalekites for what they did to Israel when they waylaid them as they came up from Egypt. Now go, attack the Amalekites and totally destroy all that belongs to them. Do not spare them; put to death men and women, children and infants, cattle and sheep, camels and donkeys."

If you think that's bad, how about the time God caused the deaths of *a few hundred thousand* firstborn babies the night before Pharaoh released God's people from captivity in Egypt?

> At midnight the LORD struck down all the firstborn in Egypt … and there was loud wailing in Egypt, for there was not a house without someone dead. (Ex. 12:29–30)

"Capricious Malevolent Bully"

Am I the only one sickened by how God killed seventy thousand innocent people because King David took a census of his troops?

> Joab reported the number of the fighting men to the king: In Israel there were eight hundred thousand able-bodied men who could handle a sword, and in Judah five hundred thousand. David was conscience-stricken after he had counted the fighting men, and he said to the LORD, "I have sinned greatly in what I have done. Now, LORD, I beg you, take away the guilt of your servant. I have done a very foolish thing." … so the LORD sent a plague on Israel from that morning until the end of the time designated, and seventy thousand of the people from Dan to Beersheba died. (2 Sam. 24:9–10, 15)

Killing seventy thousand innocent Israelites is like crop-dusting an entire town with anthrax because the governor needed to feel better about the number of officers on his police force. Think that was a one-time event? How about when:

- God killed a man for not procreating with his sister-in-law? (Gen. 38:8–10)
- God killed a man for picking up sticks on the Sabbath? (Num. 15:32–36)
- God killed seventy people for peeking inside the ark of the covenant? (1 Sam. 6:19)
- God ordered the death of three thousand people for making an idol? (Ex. 32:27–28)
- God killed 14,700 people for complaining? (Num. 16:39–49)
- God killed twenty-four thousand Israelites for the sexual sins of their army? (25:1–9)

And if those few examples weren't enough, how about the time when God annihilated everyone on the planet with a massive flood?

> Every living thing on the face of the earth was wiped out; people and animals and the creatures that move along the ground and the birds were wiped from the earth. Only Noah was left, and those with him in the ark. (Gen. 7:23)

"Bloodthirsty Ethnic Cleanser"

When I think of ethnic cleansing, I think of those killed in Bosnia or the massacres that took place in Rwanda. But before the Tutsis and Hutus made headlines, the God of the Bible called for the systematic extermination of every indigenous people group in the land of Israel. Deuteronomy chapter 7 reads like a radical Muslim cleric calling for jihad. In fact, to point out how eerily familiar this is to modern ears, read the passage below and replace every instance of "the Lord your God" with *Allah*.

> When the LORD your God brings you into the land you are entering to possess and drives out before you many nations—the Hittites, Girgashites, Amorites, Canaanites, Perizzites, Hivites … and when the LORD your God has delivered them over to you … you must destroy them totally.… Show them no mercy.… For you are a people holy to the LORD your God. The LORD your God has chosen you out of all the peoples on the face of the earth to be his people, his treasured possession. (Deut. 7:1–6)

The biblical books of Numbers, Deuteronomy, Joshua, and Judges tell the story of one long religious campaign to exterminate the indigenous people around Canaan. The actions of the Israelites read like a list of war crimes brought before the United Nations:

- Bashanites completely eradicated (Num. 21:34–35)
- Amorites slaughtered (Josh. 10:10–11)
- Seven small cities massacred (vv. 28–42)
- Twelve thousand murdered in the city of Ai (Josh. 8:1–25)

- Hazorites exterminated (11:8–12)
- Anakites exterminated (vv. 20–21)
- Ten thousand Canaanites and Perizzites slaughtered (Judg. 1:1–4)
- Ten thousand Moabites exterminated (3:28–29)
- The destruction of sixty different cities (Deut. 3:3–7)

"Vindictive"

One of the most reprehensible events of the twentieth century is what historians call the Rape of Nanking. The capital of the Republic of China, Nanking, fell to Japan on December 13, 1937. The Imperial Japanese Army unleashed a campaign of ruthless bloodshed and torture on its citizens, especially toward women. Hundreds of thousands of people died. Thousands upon thousands of women were raped, and many were taken as sex slaves.

The shocking thing is that the God you follow ordered similar atrocities perpetrated upon the Midianites, Israel's neighbors.

> The LORD said to Moses, "Take vengeance on the Midianites for the Israelites. After that, you will be gathered to your people."…They fought against Midian, as the LORD commanded Moses, and killed every man.…
>
> The Israelites captured the Midianite women and children and took all the Midianite herds, flocks and goods as plunder. They burned all the

> towns where the Midianites had settled, as well as all their camps. They took all the plunder and spoils, including the people and animals, and brought the captives, spoils and plunder to Moses and Eleazar the priest and the Israelite assembly at their camp on the plains of Moab, by the Jordan across from Jericho. Moses, Eleazar the priest and all the leaders of the community went to meet them outside the camp.
>
> Moses was angry with the officers of the army—the commanders of thousands and commanders of hundreds—who returned from the battle. "Have you allowed all the women to live?" he asked them. "They were the ones who followed Balaam's advice and enticed the Israelites to be unfaithful to the LORD in the Peor incident, so that a plague struck the LORD's people. Now kill all the boys. And kill every woman who has slept with a man, but save for yourselves every girl who has never slept with a man." (Num. 31:1–2, 7, 9–18)

NEW TESTAMENT EXAMPLES

As you read, you might be thinking, *God changed the way He dealt with His people after Jesus rose from the dead and inaugurated the new covenant. That's just the Old Testament. God doesn't treat people like that in the New Testament.*

Really?

How about the time when a couple named Ananias and Sapphira claimed to be more sacrificial than they really were, and as a result were struck dead on the spot (Acts 5:1–10)?

How about the warning the apostle Paul gave to the Christians in the ancient Greek city of Corinth? He instructed them to take the Lord's Supper with the utmost seriousness or some might die as a result: "That is why many among you are weak and sick, and a number of you have fallen asleep" (1 Cor. 11:30).

How about the ghastly warning to the community of believers in the ancient Turkish town of Thyatira?

> Nevertheless, I have this against you: You tolerate that woman Jezebel, who calls herself a prophet. By her teaching she misleads my servants into sexual immorality and the eating of food sacrificed to idols. I have given her time to repent of her immorality, but she is unwilling. So I will cast her on a bed of suffering, and I will make those who commit adultery with her suffer intensely, unless they repent of her ways. I will strike her children dead. Then all the churches will know that I am he who searches hearts and minds, and I will repay each of you according to your deeds. (Rev. 2:20–23)

Killing church members who fall into sexual immorality as a way to remind Christians that God repays people according to their deeds? Causing people who inappropriately take the Lord's Supper to fall into cardiac arrest? Killing donors during a capital campaign because they exaggerated their giving?

The brutal wrath of the Lord our God is the same in the Old Testament and the New Testament. Same God. Same wrath. Same character. God is the same, yesterday, today, and forever (Heb. 13:8). He does not change (Mal. 3:6; James 1:17).

THE REAL ISSUE

Why do I bring up Scriptures that cast God in an unflattering light? Why bring up situations that might cast doubt on the goodness of God? Why go to great lengths to describe how utterly loathsome God can be in a book designed to motivate Christians to share their faith with their non-Christian friends?

My answer is simple: Apocalyptic urgency is not about saving your friend from hell. It's about saving your friend *from God*. Hell isn't your lost friend's biggest problem; *God is*. Hell is simply the end result of God's justified wrath. It's the final permanent expression of His anger toward those who have purposely chosen to reject His lordship over their lives.

That's why until you understand how violent and inhumane God really is, how utterly wrathful the God and Father of our Lord Jesus Christ can become, you'll never feel the urgency to help your non-Christian friends escape His detestable clutches.

Hebrews 10:31 says, "It is a dreadful thing to fall into the hands of the living God."

That has to be the biggest understatement in all of Scripture.

NOTES

1. Søren Kierkegaard, *Attack Upon "Christendom,"* trans. Water Lowrie (Princeton, NJ: Princeton University Press, 1968), 279.

2. Colin Brown, ed., *The New International Dictionary of New Testament Theology* (Grand Rapids, MI: Regency Reference Library, 1986), 1:107.

3. Gerhard Kittel and Gerhard Friedrich, eds., trans. Geoffrey W. Bromiley, *Theological Dictionary of the New Testament, Abridged* (Grand Rapids, MI: Eerdmans, 1985), 717.

4. Douglas Moo, *The Epistle to the Romans* (Grand Rapids, MI: Eerdmans, 1996), 101.

5. Ibid, 99.

6. Richard Dawkins, *The God Delusion* (New York: Houghton Mifflin Harcourt, 2008), 51.

7
PROPITIATION

This is God's universe, and He is doing things His way. You may think you have a better way, but you don't have a universe.

—J. Vernon McGee[1]

Fourth grade was a life-altering school year for me. This was the year I realized not everyone believed the same way I did about God. It was also the year I saw a woman's naked breasts for the very first time, and it wasn't until much later in life that I realized that the second experience led to the first.

Our teacher, Mrs. Byrd, was a short, older woman, with a large wart perched on her left nostril, a wart that seemed to stare at you whenever you approached her desk with a question. Her volatile temper was equaled only by her utter lack of classroom-management skills. Looking back, she was the kind of bitter and frazzled teacher you'd expect to see in a Hollywood movie. She was also the ideal target for a fourth grade boy's mischief.

I'll never forget the day Donny Martin played the greatest prank in the history of Kae Avenue Elementary. Donny sneaked into our classroom during recess and secretly taped a *Playboy* centerfold picture inside the map of North and South America. If you're as old as I am, you probably remember having maps at the front of your classroom that rolled up into a tube until the teacher pulled the map down for the class to see. It created a perfect setup for Donny's trick.

We studied geography on Tuesdays and Thursdays, right after recess. Mrs. Byrd would slowly hobble over to the map, turn to the class as she pulled the string to unroll it, and declare, "Children, it's time for geography." Only this day, as she unrolled the map, it wasn't two sets of continents staring back at us.

At first Mrs. Byrd didn't notice the centerfold as she faced the class. We saw the picture but sat in stunned silence, especially the boys. After a few moments, our poor unsuspecting teacher turned around and muttered in her monotonous voice, "Class, today I want you to notice that—" and then catching sight of the bare-chested woman, she screamed, "O-H D-E-A-R G-O-D I-N H-E-A-V-E-N!" She steadied herself against the wall with her hand, ripped the picture off the map, and bolted to the principal's office. The class erupted in laughter. Donny stood up and took a bow. The next day we had a substitute teacher. And when Mrs. Byrd came back, she was never able to regain control of our classroom again.

I had never seen a naked woman before that day, and as much as that was a pleasantly curious experience for a fourth-grade boy, the moment was overshadowed by what followed. In the wake of Mrs. Byrd losing control of the class, something profound happened—the students actually started to talk with one another. With our necks no longer facing forward all day long, lively discussions erupted all over the place. As it turned out, we taught ourselves things that year that poor old Mrs. Byrd never could. And for that I am eternally grateful.

Fourth grade was the year I realized that not everyone believed in God like I did. It was the year my friend Jimmy Bickle threw down a theological gauntlet, as our classroom line leaders formed two lines to go down to the Christmas program in the gymnasium. Jimmy shot out of his desk like a Hebrew prophet of old and defiantly proclaimed, "I am Jewish. I am proud of this fact. I do not believe in Jesus, and I am *not* going to participate in the Christmas special this year!"

Jimmy's outburst triggered an ongoing discussion about religion that lasted until the end of that school year. After the Christmas program, a group of us stood around the dodgeball court and asked, "Jimmy's Jewish. What religion are you?"

I told everyone I was a Christian because that's what my parents were.

"Yeah, but what *kind* of Christian are you?" someone asked.

We attended a non-denominational church. I didn't know.

"Uh, I think I'm just a Christian," I told them.

"Yeah, but *what kind* of Christian?" another asked.

Eventually, just to get them off my back, I blurted out, "I'm a Presbyterian." I had absolutely no idea what that meant. I had seen it on a church sign somewhere.

During that year I noticed Wendy, the most beautiful nine-year-old girl in the world. I passed Wendy's house every day when I walked to and from school. She had seven brothers and sisters, wore a special uniform to school, and rode a bus to another school across town. One afternoon as we climbed up into her tree house, I tried to hold her hand, but she pushed my arm away.

"My mom said I can only like boys who are Catholics."

"What's a Catholic?" I asked.

She said it was her religion.

I awkwardly responded, "Well, I want to be a Catholic too!"

At end of fourth grade, Kelly Shockerman moved into the house next to Wendy. I liked going over to his house because his dad was a scientist who worked in the ocean, so their family had tanks full of exotic fish throughout his house. One day I asked Kelly if he could go to vacation Bible school with me. His parents told him that their family didn't believe in God, so he wasn't allowed to go. I was shocked. I thought everyone believed in God.

All of this newfound talk about God, rules, and religion was upsetting to me. It was as if my entire fourth-grade class had been enjoying the day, taking an afternoon stroll together, and then all of a sudden we turned a corner and bullets flew everywhere as the adults in our lives attacked one another's beliefs. Confused and completely unaware of what was actually happening, one by one we started choosing sides.

It seemed so unnatural, and so unnecessary. Why choose sides at all? Aren't we all talking about the same God anyway, just with different names and ways of relating to Him? We were getting along just fine until this religion business crept up on us. There we were—black, white, Asian, Hispanic, rich, and poor—and none of these things mattered to us. Then along came religion. It divided us, caused us to choose sides, and forced us to label one another. And I resented it.

BEYOND A FOURTH-GRADE MIND-SET

In 1971 John Lennon released his song "Imagine," considered one of the most popular songs ever written:

> *Imagine there's no heaven*
> . . .
> *No hell below us*
> *Above us only sky*
> *Imagine all the people*
> *Living for today.*[2]

Whenever I hear that song, my mind goes back to Kae Avenue Elementary School. I think about my friends in Mrs. Byrd's fourth-grade class before religion started to divide us. We felt free, unencumbered, and full of joy. "Imagine" makes me think of walking down the hall with Diane Miller to the library. It evokes the excitement I felt in Mr. Bline's gym class. "Imagine" stirs up the feelings we had before religion messed everything up—freedom, possibility, and limitless wonder.

When the song ends, another thought hits me: Fourth graders would eat ice cream every day if we let them.

Or stay up until 2:00 a.m. watching Nickelodeon.

Or skip brushing their teeth altogether.

Or never do chores around the house.

Or constantly fight with their siblings.

Why? Because they're fourth graders! They have no responsibilities. They're kids. I've had fourth graders, three of them to be exact. They were great kids at that age, but their world wasn't real.

It was childhood, a time of suspended pressure and responsibility. Childhood is *supposed* to be magical, unencumbered, and full of joy, just like I experienced it. But it isn't supposed to be permanent. It is a phase we enjoy fleetingly during the transition from infancy to adulthood.

There's another reason "Imagine" makes me think of Mrs. Byrd's class—it was written by a hashish-smoking billionaire who lived life like a fourth grader.

People like you and I, we live in the real world. We live in a place where people have to grow up, make difficult decisions, get jobs, and work hard. Part of growing up is moving beyond John Lennon's fourth-grade Utopian mentality. It's about moving past the desire to sit around and smoke pot all day and try to live lives of unending bliss and happiness. The difference between a fourth grader and an adult is real life, the place where cars won't start, spouses aren't always faithful, and people have to choose between paying for health insurance or groceries.

In the real world people make radically important decisions all the time: Should I marry him? Should I take that job? Should we have kids? Move to that state? Take this treatment? We're used to it because that's what adults do. And it's in this real world that people begin asking questions like, "Why am I here? How do I find my place in the universe? Are we alone? Is there a Being that created all of this?"

It's at this point—the point when we human beings start asking questions about meaning and transcendence—that people raised in the Western culture and its worldviews want to think like fourth graders instead of like adults.

Above all else, these days people want to live in a world without religious bickering. And that's completely understandable. I hate bickering. But if there's an ultimate truth out there to govern our lives, that truth, just like the other truths we learn in life, must be found. Questions have to be asked. Evidence must be weighed. This search involves discussion, debate, and even disagreement. That's how we find truth.

The problem is that we live in a culture where people want to avoid honest discussions about religion. The forces of our culture convince people to long for a simpler time—like fourth grade at Kae Avenue Elementary—a time free of religious disagreement and division.

The reality is that *I want* to live like religion doesn't matter too; I want to live like what I actually believe isn't that important. I like being liked. I don't like making waves. I don't like making people feel awkward. But I can't back down from what I know to be true. Sheer logic will not let me do that. Like the atheist philosopher Bertrand Russell, Christians have always known there can't be more than one correct religion.

> I think all the great religions of the world—Buddhism, Hinduism, Christianity, Islam, and Communism—both untrue and harmful. It is evident as a matter of logic that, since they disagree, not more than one of them can be true.[3]

More importantly, for two thousand years, most Christians have rejected the "don't ask/don't tell" religious mold into which our culture has consistently tried to pour us. Not surprising, even in the most persecution-filled environments, Christians have always been willing to share their faith. We've always felt it better to risk causing division than to not get the gospel message out.

Why?

Because there is something unique about Christianity that not only sets it apart from *all* other religions, but drives Christians to the point of martyrdom to help their non-Christian friends and family discover it.

Do you know what that is?

Below you'll find the names of a tiny fraction of the religions in the world, both past and present. I want you to read them and ask yourself, "What is so important about Christianity that it's worth offending the people who lovingly and authentically embrace these and thousands of other religions?" What is it about our faith that forces us to abandon the immense cultural drive to act like fourth graders when it comes to religion?"

Take a look:

> Ananda Marga, Cheondoism, Shinto, Bahá'í, Dhammakaya movement, Hinduism, Shingon Buddhism, Orphism, I-Kuan Tao, Dharma-character school, Gaelic mythology, Arya Samaj, Mormonism, Quimbanda, Rastafari movement, Hasidic Judaism, Manichaeism, Deobandi, Alevi, Lakota mythology, Jainism, Ash'ari, Confucianism, Santería, Mithraism, Scientology, Maori mythology, Konkokyo, Shia Islam, New Age, Vaishnavism,

Yogācāra, Sufism, Zoroastrianism, Anito, Zulu mythology, and Hermeticism.

Let me ask that question again: What is so important about Christianity that it's worth offending the billions upon billions of people who lovingly and authentically embrace these and many other religions? What makes it worth risking misunderstanding, awkwardness, losing a friendship, and even losing your life?

The answer is simple. It's one word: *propitiation.*

As helpful, insightful, and meaningful as other religious systems can seem, none of them, and I mean *none* of them, can provide the means to propitiate the wrath of God.

WHAT IS PROPITIATION?

When Jesus died on the cross, what happened exactly? Have you ever thought about that? I mean He died, obviously. That's a given. But what is the significance of His death? What happened on the cross two thousand years ago that has a much larger significance than the simple death of an itinerant peasant teacher?

Christians have always maintained that something more happened than just Jesus' heart stopping and His body dying. To Christians, Jesus' death was a part of God's larger plan for Himself, for you, and for me. His execution accomplished something of eternal importance. It wasn't an accident. It was a planned event meant to accomplish a specific purpose.

Theologians use various words to describe what Jesus' death on the cross accomplished. Each of these words illuminates a unique aspect of what happened on the cross at Calvary two thousand years ago.

Redemption

The term *redemption* conveys the idea of being "bought back." If a thief steals an expensive watch, sells it to a pawn shop, and then the original owner goes and pays a large sum of money to buy it back—that's an example of redemption. Jesus' death served as God's payment to "buy us back" from sin, darkness, the Devil, and hell (Col. 1:14).

Reconciliation

The term *reconciliation* conveys the idea of two people whose relationship was damaged, and they became enemies before later coming back together. Jesus' death restores humanity's broken relationship with God (Rom. 5:11).

Substitute Atonement

The term *substitute atonement* conveys the idea of someone stepping up to take upon himself or herself the punishment due another person. Jesus, in His death, stepped up to take the punishment we deserved because of our sin (Isa. 53:5).

Like looking at a diamond from various angles, the death of Jesus has multiple meanings and many layers. But there is one aspect of Jesus' death that is more central than all the others combined, and that's the idea of propitiation. It's what theologian J. I. Packer calls "the heart of the gospel."[4]

Propitiation

Propitiation is "an offering that turns away *wrath*."[5] Jesus' death on the cross served as a sacrificial offering that appeased God's wrath and opened up the possibility for people to spend eternity with Him in heaven (Rom. 3:25).

Admittedly, propitiation is a crude and barbaric concept. In fact, to make sure you understand how distasteful propitiation really is, I want you to picture this scene:

> Imagine an island in the South Pacific, completely cut off from modern-day civilization. Formed from volcanic activity, the island experiences frequent tremors, earthquakes, and a continuous stream of smoke billowing from the live volcano in the center of the island.
>
> One day as thc islanders feel the volcanic rumblings underneath their feet, they become convinced that someone's sinfulness has angered the island god. To avert potential island-wide disaster, a representative is chosen to present an offering to appease the god's wrath. The humble servant, head bowed, walks into the temple, carrying a goat tucked under his arm.
>
> Once inside he unsheathes a large knife, slits the animal's throat, and lays the blood-soaked animal on the altar before the island god. Smoke and fire shoot out from the altar. Loud cracks of thunder shake the room. The temple floor rumbles underneath the islander's feet.
>
> Shocked that he is still alive after delivering the sacrifice, the lowly islander walks backward

> out of the temple, retracing his steps, arched over, face to the ground, never once making eye contact with the deity.
>
> Now alone with the sacrifice, the angry god focuses his eyes on the offering, weighs the expense and thoughtfulness that went into making the gift, and deems the sacrifice worthy enough to appease his wrath.
>
> The deity, duly honored by the worthiness of the sacrifice, slowly calms himself down and calls off all retribution he had planned for the islanders. Peace is restored on the island and the earthquakes and tremors cease.

That's the concept of propitiation. Propitiation is barbaric. Most people are surprised to discover that not only does the Bible talk about the idea of propitiation, but the apostle Paul uses the image to convey the central meaning behind the crucifixion of Jesus.

JESUS' DEATH OFFERING

The clearest teaching in Scripture about propitiation is Romans 3:25–26:

> God presented Christ as a sacrifice of atonement, through the shedding of his blood—to be received by faith. He did this to demonstrate his righteousness, because in his forbearance he had left the sins committed beforehand unpunished—

> he did it to demonstrate his righteousness at the present time, so as to be just and the one who justifies those who have faith in Jesus.

"Sacrifice of atonement" is a translation of the Greek word *hilasterion*, which ancient Greeks used to describe "a propitiatory gift for the gods."[6] The older translations of the Bible such as the King James, American Standard, and New American Standard versions all used the word *propitiation* as a translation of *hilasterion,* while newer English translations have opted to translate it with phrases like "sacrifice of atonement" or "sacrifice for sin." The meaning is the same, regardless.

Hilasterion was used to describe offerings made in pagan temples. Surprisingly, Paul chose this exact word to capture the essence of the work of Christ on the cross. One must not think, however, that every aspect of the pagan act of propitiation was what the apostle Paul had in mind.

In fact, there are two things that differentiate the Christian understanding of propitiation from its pagan counterparts.

1. Justice vs. Impulsive Rage

Twice in Romans 3:25–26 Paul tells us that God presented Christ as a propitiation "to demonstrate his justice."[7] There is an immense difference between biblical justice and the pagan image of an angry Zeus needing a worthy sacrifice to reassure him that his followers truly love and respect him. It's as vast as the difference between the way a serial killer murders a victim and the way a judge sentences that same serial killer to death. Both scenarios involve causing someone's death, but one is the result of unrestrained carnal rage, and the other emanates from satisfying the demands of justice.

The biblical idea of propitiation is rooted in the character of God. Propitiation is needed, not because God is angry, *but because God is holy*. Wrath is simply God's response to the presence of sin. Sin and a holy God cannot coexist in the same universe, let alone in the same room. Since God obviously will not change, the sinner must. The two options are either God causes the sinful person to be permanently "shut out from the presence of the Lord" in hell (2 Thess. 1:9), or He satisfies the demands of His holiness another way. Propitiation is that second option. Propitiation satisfies God's need for holy justice. In effect, as theologian Jack Cottrell points out, at the cross Jesus "suffered the equivalent of eternity in hell for every sinner."[8]

2. "God Presented"

The major way biblical propitiation is different from the pagan concept is in the nature of the gift itself. Romans 3:25 begins by saying, "God presented Christ." That's a loaded phrase. In biblical propitiation, a sacrificial gift isn't offered because a sinful person thinks, *You know, I think I need to offer a sacrifice to God to appease His wrath.* Biblical propitiation was God's idea. God realized the need for it, and more importantly, He provided the gift Himself. In fact, to be more specific, God *became* the gift.

The Roman poet Horace advised his fellow playwrights, "Do not bring a god on to the stage unless the problem is one that deserves a god to solve it."[9] By the turn of the first millennium sin had so badly distorted God's plot for humanity that the time to "bring a God on stage" had finally come.

Throughout the history of the Jewish nation, God's people offered their sacrifices to an offended God. Through prayers, tears, and animal sacrifices, propitiation after propitiation was made to appease God's wrath. But as Romans 3:25 makes clear, before Jesus' death "he had left the sins committed beforehand unpunished." None of these sacrifices, however purely motivated, could completely appease God's wrath against human sin.

After centuries of inadequate attempts by God's people to satisfy His holy nature, a God was finally brought onto the stage. "When the set time had fully come, God sent his Son, born of a woman, born under the law, to redeem those under the law" (Gal. 4:4–5).

Animal sacrifices had become ineffective.

Human prayers and penance were wholly inadequate.

The time for a *human* sacrifice had arrived, but not just any human being could be sacrificed. It had to be a perfect human being, someone without sin.

But none were available.

No human had ever (or would ever) live a perfectly sinless life and become the ideal candidate. Out of options, God's solution was both simple and bizarre: Since God was the only being without sin in the universe, He Himself, motivated by reckless, unstoppable love, would enter time and space as a human being and become the propitiatory sacrifice that would appease His own wrath.

"This is love," the apostle John wrote. "Not that we loved God, but that he loved us and sent his Son as an atoning sacrifice (*hilasterion*) for our sins" (1 John 4:10).

This truly is the heart of the gospel.

NOT ENOUGH

A few years ago a Christian woman approached me after one of our Easter services and came completely uncorked on me.

"You don't get it do you?" she yelled. "I've visited your church every Easter for three years and every time, and I mean *every time*, you talk about how Jesus was brutally killed and then brought back to life. Death. Blood. Violence. Wrath. *Enough already!*"

I paused, then with raised eyebrows said, "Um, it's Easter. That's what Easter is about. What would you like me to talk about?"

She sighed, pointed to her daughter's pink Easter dress and said, "Look at this—pink dresses, Easter eggs, little bunnies, and family dinners with Grandma. That's what Easter is about."

After reading this you may be right where she's at—struggling to reconcile what you've believed to be the point of Christianity and this whole business of propitiation. I completely understand. It's a hard thing to wrap your mind around.

If you're having a hard time stomaching what *truly* lies at the core of Christian belief (propitiation), you're starting to grasp, if only in small measure, how truly strange Christianity really is.

Christianity is a beautifully disturbing religion at its core. Not because God is barbaric. Not because Christianity is steeped in a superstitious worldview. Rather, because sin is a repulsive thing to behold, especially for a perfect God. Yet, for all the bloodshed, propitiation emanates from God's immense love for His creation. As Leon Morris points out, "It is the combination of God's deep love for the sinner with His uncompromising reaction against sin which brings about what the Bible calls propitiation."[10]

Herein lies the beginning of apocalyptic urgency.

When I say that propitiation separates Christianity from every single religion on the planet, what I'm saying is that Christianity claims that Jesus Himself became a *death offering* to God that was deemed *enough;* it was enough of an offering to appease God and dissipate His holy wrath. In other words, it worked. It did the job. The slaughter of Jesus pleased God.

Before Jesus was butchered and laid before God to divert His wrath, we were toast. It was over and our fates were sealed. Our destiny in hell was already decided.

After Jesus' death everything changed. God was pleased with the sacrifice and His wrath was averted. It was enough. That can't be said about non-Christian religions. All of them are inadequate. None provide enough of a sacrifice to bring God back into a right frame of mind so that He doesn't ultimately punish those religions' followers with His wrath in hell.

In fact, just to reinforce this even more, I'd like for you to do something. From now on whenever you hear the name of a religion other than Christianity, I want you to picture the words *not enough* in parentheses after the name:

> Judaism (*not enough*)
> Buddhism (*not enough*)
> Jainism (*not enough*)
> Islam (*not enough*)
> Vaishnavism (*not enough*)

Jesus' slaughter *was enough* to cover our sins so God could be in our presence without instantaneously destroying us. Following the basic tenets of Islam can't do that for you. You could be a faithful Muslim who believes there is no God but Allah, that Muhammad is his messenger, you could pray five times a day, fast during Ramadan, give alms to the poor, and make the pilgrimage to Mecca. You could do all that and more, and it still wouldn't be enough to appease God's wrath.

In fact, the sum total of the offering presented to God by following Islam is so insufficient that you could make fifty million trips to Mecca, give every single dime of your wealth to the poor, pray fifteen hundred times a day for the rest of your life, and it still wouldn't be enough.

Even if you felt better as a person adhering to those beliefs.

Even if those beliefs gave your life meaning and purpose.

Even if those beliefs rescued you from a life-controlling addiction.

Even if those beliefs saved your marriage.

Even if you think those beliefs are the hope of the world.

Those beliefs are simply *not enough.*

And that's not a statement against Islam so much as it's a statement about *all* non-Christian religions.

Again, think about the other religions, philosophies, and traditions of the world and the countless men and women who sincerely place their faith in them. What is it about Christianity that makes it worth offending these people by saying their sincerity is *not enough?* What is worth risking awkward conversations, strained or broken relationships, and even your own safety? What causes a Christian to be mildly committed to evangelism one day and the next day consumed with apocalyptic urgency to reach his or her friends for Christ?

One word: *propitiation*.

They finally "get" what Jesus' death on the cross really accomplished. But still, this isn't what creates apocalyptic urgency.

What grabs our hearts with the force of eternity is the moment we realize that, as Romans 3:25 says, "God presented Christ as a sacrifice of atonement, through the shedding of his blood—*to be received by faith*."

The benefits of Christ's propitiation must "be received by faith." That means friends and family members have to know they are "deserving of wrath" (Eph. 2:3), and they must understand the mess they're in before they can do something about it.

They must be told by *someone wearing skin*.

And that someone is you.

BREAKING THE SILENCE

While I certainly have aspects of my life that need work, there is one constant in my weekly routine that I can look forward to that is nearly perfect: Once a week, I frequent the single greatest Chinese restaurant in the history of human civilization. If you're ever in town, swing by and I'll take you there. Within minutes you'll agree with me.

If I took you there, and we were able to actually get a seat right away, you'd probably point to the amazing sauce that they put on their sesame chicken as the secret to their success. No place anywhere, in any city, any place on the planet, can match the sauce. I've checked. There is a universal principle understood by all professional connoisseurs of Chinese food: You either "get" sesame chicken sauce, or you don't. There is no "try" with sesame chicken sauce. Either the sesame chicken sauce gods have magically bestowed their secrets upon you, or they haven't.

The spring rolls are to die for. The sweet and sour chicken is unparalleled. People stand in line forever to order take-out Mongolian beef and shrimp lo mein.

But as amazing as the food is, that's not why people keep going back to this particular restaurant. People in our town swamp this little hole-in-the-wall Chinese restaurant, not because of the food, but because of the owners—Tony and Shelly (as they are known by their chosen American names). They call you by name when you walk in. They remember the names of your spouse and your kids. Their personal interest in their customers isn't some technique they picked up at a Dale Carnegie seminar. They actually do care, deeply.

They personally greet you at the door when you arrive, walk by your table two to three times during your meal to personally check on things, and shake your hand on the way out. People love to be loved, and as anyone in our area knows, love is the best thing on their menu.

Over the years I've come to know Tony and Shelly quite well. Both were born and raised in China, came to the United States in their twenties, and have worked hard to speak the language, fit into their adopted country, and pursue their dream of running a great restaurant.

Tony always works hard to carry on a conversation with me in his broken English. Every time he speaks I sense his frustration with the limits of his language skills. He's an extreme extrovert. If he were speaking in his native Mandarin, I'm sure I'd never get a word in edgewise.

What's special about Tony and Shelly is that every summer they send their two kids back to China to stay with their grandparents. "Very, very important to learn Chinese culture," Tony tells me. While in China their kids hone their Mandarin language skills, reconnect with their family, and go on various cultural excursions. It's an annual reintroduction to the culture *and* the religion that Tony and Shelly hold dear.

And therein lies my greatest struggle.

As a Christ follower who stumbled into their restaurant by accident one day, just happened to develop a friendship with the owner, and who is naturally quite timid when it comes to sharing my faith—I don't want to talk to my Buddhist friend Tony about Jesus.

I don't want to risk ruining this nice friendship we have going. It might be awkward. He could be offended. He might misconstrue my attempts to explain the unbelievable good news of Christianity as a cultural slap in his face. I understand the risks. The risks are real.

But there's one thing I know that Tony doesn't:

Buddhism is *not enough.*

And while I'd like to pretend that I can be a faithful follower of Jesus and live my life like a fourth grader, never rocking the relational boat and keeping everyone happy, there is one thing about which I am absolutely confident: Tony is a genuinely loving person, and if he knew what I knew, I know he'd risk our friendship to tell me about it.

NOTES

1. J. Vernon McGee, *Ephesians* (Nashville: Thomas Nelson, 1991), 76.

2. John Lennon, "Imagine," *Imagine* studio album, recorded 23 June–5 July, 1971, in New York, Apple, EMI.

3. Bertrand Russell, *Why I Am Not a Christian* (New York: Simon & Schuster, 1957), v.

4. J. I. Packer, *Knowing God* (Downer's Grove, IL: InterVarsity Press, 1973), 163.

5. Jack Cottrell, *The Faith Once for All* (Joplin, MO: College Press), 265.

6. Colin Brown, ed., *The New International Dictionary of New Testament Theology* (Grand Rapids, MI: Regency Reference Library, 1986), 3:149.

7. This verse is from the 1984 translation of the New International Version.

8. Cottrell, *The Faith Once for All*, 267.

9. Horace, *Ars Poetica* 131 f., quoted in F. F. Bruce, *Romans* (Grand Rapids, MI: Eerdmans, 1985), 96.

10. Leon Morris, *The Apostolic Preaching of the Cross* (Grand Rapids, MI: Eerdmans, 1987), 210.

8
SKIN

The gospel is only good news if it gets there in time.

—Carl F. H. Henry[1]

My first day in seminary I got a job working in the seminary bookstore, only to be fired three weeks later for "evangelizing the students."

Yeah, you read that right.

I was *fired* from a *seminary* bookstore.

For *evangelizing* students preparing to be pastors.

When I enrolled at Princeton Theological Seminary, I knew the school wasn't exactly a bastion of evangelical Christianity. However, nothing could have prepared me for the absolute disregard many of the students had for the authority of Scripture. It was shocking, actually.

At the bookstore I processed the books shipped through the mail and then placed them on the store shelves for sale. Like every job I've ever had, I arrived early, stayed late, worked hard, and tried to add value in any way I could.

To pass time, the five or six of us (all students) who worked in the back would talk for hours as we unpacked books, affixed price tags, and carried them out to the shelves. It was one of those "I'm so bored I'm going to rip my eyeballs out of my head if I have to do this any longer" kind of jobs, so we talked to pass the time.

My first day was telling. I met a young woman preparing to be a pastor who had just spent the weekend in a nonstop drunken stupor.

"You spent the whole weekend getting smashed?" I asked her. "Wait, aren't you preparing to be a pastor?"

"Yeah, but it was an incredible party."

"Oh. Okay."

After a few minutes, another student told me out of the blue that she was a lesbian.

"I see you have a ring on. How long have you been married?" she asked me.

"Three years in July," I said.

"My girlfriend and I have been together for three years too. She's coming to visit this weekend."

Not quite sure how to respond, I said, "Oh, that's nice."

A guy sitting across from me introduced himself and asked me what my long-term goals were in ministry.

"I feel called to start a new church somewhere. I'd also like to teach in a Christian college as an adjunct professor."

"So you're obviously conservative."

"Well, I wouldn't put a label on it. I'm—"

"But you feel like you have the right to force your opinions about God on other people, right?"

"Well, no, I don't … I mean … if I was … um … *what?*"

"I just think evangelism is spiritually oppressing people."

"But we're all preparing to be pastors in churches!" I said. "The last time I checked, Jesus' command to evangelize the world hasn't been retracted."

"You're a fundamentalist."

"No, I'm not."

"Yes, you are."

"No, I'm not."

"Yes, you are."

"What, are we like in third grade now, resorting to name-calling?" I shot back. The conversations that first day set the tone for the rest of my three weeks at the bookstore. Each day I found myself drawn into wild conversations about Marxist Liberation theology, the Buddhist-Christian dialogue, and the ordination of homosexuals. These discussions were all new to me. And fascinating. Yet I found, time and time again, that I was the only one asking the question, "What does the Bible say about this?"

Over time I grew weary of the debates, so when the topic of religion came up, I simply talked about my relationship with Christ—what He meant to me, and how He continued to change my heart. I felt certain that I wasn't as smart as these people, but I could love them and help them grow spiritually. I figured that's really why we came to seminary anyway, to prepare ourselves for spiritual leadership in the church.

Then something happened. After about three weeks, the manager of the bookstore abruptly called me into her office.

"Brian, this is just not working out."

"Not working out? I work harder than all your other employees combined."

"Yeah, but you're evangelizing the students."

"Evangelizing the students? We're all Christians! How can you evangelize people who already claim to be Christ followers?"

"I just think you make people feel uncomfortable."

"You mean we can have a heated three-hour discussion about the spirituality of Che Guevara (the Argentine Marxist revolutionary), but if I mention Jesus, and what He's doing in my life, that's out of line?"

"Yes."

"That's ridiculous. This is a Christian seminary bookstore."

"I don't care. I'm the manager and I say that this is an evangelism-free environment."

"But we're all Christians. You can't evangelize people who are already Christians!"

"Doesn't matter. I've made my decision. I'm firing you."

"You're firing me?"

"Yes."

"You're *seriously* firing me for talking about my faith in a seminary bookstore?"

"Yep."

"You know this has to be a first in the history of, well, the entire Christian religion."

"I don't care. I can't have people running around here trying to convert people. I just don't think that's something Jesus wants us to do."

"You're serious?"

"Like a heart attack."

"I'm being fired."

"Right now."

"Because I *evangelized* seminary students?"

"Yep."

And that was that.

I walked out the door, fired, for the first and only time in my life.

EVANGELISM EXCUSES

As absurd as getting fired seemed at the time, it made perfect sense once I acclimated to the rest of the seminary environment. I described one of my professors in a previous chapter. What I haven't shared yet is that one of my New Testament Greek professors was open about being a lesbian. My Pauline Epistles professor often came to class quite tipsy and randomly swore at the students in the class. And my Church History professor would often crassly ask my friends and me, "Gentlemen, did you screw any women this weekend?" Not the kind of environment you'd expect to raise up powerful men and women of God to go out and change the world.

Of course, I don't want to give you the wrong idea. There were some amazing Christlike professors and students there too. But unfortunately, as often happens, "A little yeast works through the whole batch of dough" (Gal. 5:9). The influence of the misdirected few disproportionately drowned out the influence of the rest of the campus.

I bring all of this up to say one thing: It's not surprising at all that the vast majority of the students with whom I went to seminary felt no passion whatsoever to reach nonbelievers with the gospel. That's not shocking at all. If whoever teaches you about Christianity erodes the trustworthiness of Scripture, all kinds of bizarre beliefs and lifestyle choices follow.

What *is* shocking to me is the number of Bible-believing Christians I've known over the last twenty-five years who were equally adamant about not sharing their faith, just for different reasons. Have you ever heard Bible-believing Christians give the following explanations as to why they don't actively share their faith?

> "I don't have the gift of evangelism. God has given me other gifts."
> "I need to focus on my own spiritual growth right now."
> "I don't know enough about the Bible yet."
> "Evangelism is God's job."

What do all of these statements have in common?

They're used by lots of Bible-believing Christians. These excuses sound very spiritual. They appear to be the kinds of things super-devout Christ followers would say, if for no other reason than lots of Christians who try to appear superdevout have repeated these phrases over the years.

And one more thing: They're all dead wrong.

They are a gross distortion of biblical truth.

GOD'S PART AND OUR PART IN EVANGELISM

Christians who believe the Bible is God's authoritative Word but still refuse to evangelize are often confused about the part God plays in the evangelistic process and the part they are required to play. The apostle Paul spells out these two aspects of the evangelism process perfectly in 2 Corinthians 5:17–21:

> Therefore, if anyone is in Christ, the new creation has come: The old has gone, the new is here! All this

> is from God, who reconciled us to himself through Christ and gave us the ministry of reconciliation: that God was reconciling the world to himself in Christ, not counting people's sins against them. And he has committed to us the message of reconciliation. We are therefore Christ's ambassadors, as though God were making his appeal through us. We implore you on Christ's behalf: Be reconciled to God. God made him who had no sin to be sin for us, so that in him we might become the righteousness of God.

God's Part

God played His part in the evangelistic process by reconciling non-Christians "to himself through Christ" (v. 18). The cross was God's job. It is a finished work. What most Christians fail to understand, however, is that the cross created the *possibility* of reconciliation. Every nonbeliever on the planet wasn't immediately reconciled to God the day Jesus died. As Romans 3:25 says, "God presented Christ as a sacrifice of atonement, through the shedding of his blood—*to be received by faith*." The benefits of propitiation (i.e., wrath deflected, forgiveness, etc.) can only be received when one places his or her faith and trust in Christ.

Our Part

Our part is as important as God's part. Our job is to share with people "the good news" of Jesus' work on the cross and persuade them to apply it to their lives. Paul said that God "gave us the ministry of reconciliation" (2 Cor. 5:18). God's part is the cross. Our part is helping friends and family members who are "deserving of [God's] wrath" (Eph. 2:3) reconcile with God. Both parts work together in tandem.

Notice the phrase "God gave us" (see 2 Cor. 5:18). God didn't ask if we might be interested in helping Him at some point when we have free time. He didn't suggest that it might be nice to share in what He did through Jesus, but only if we could work it into our schedules. The Creator of the universe "gave us the ministry of reconciliation" (v. 18).

Admittedly, you didn't ask for this.

You may not want to be involved.

You may not even like it.

But it's your ministry now.

God gave it to you.

NO EXCUSES

"I don't have the gift of evangelism" and other statements like it are just excuses, and none of them has the support of Scripture. Christians say these things when they want to get off the hook from the responsibility to share their faith with their nonbelieving friends.

If you use these types of excuses to justify your lack of evangelistic passion and action, I guarantee that other nonevangelistic Christians will overhear you and help you justify your disobedience.

Regardless of how many years they've been Christians or how extensively they claim to know the Bible—they're lying to you. If you're not sharing your faith and you feel bad about yourself, *that's a good thing.*

When Peter tried to deter Jesus from going to the cross, Jesus said, "Get behind me, Satan! You are a stumbling block to me; you do not have in mind the concerns of God, but merely human concerns" (Matt. 16:23).

There are *no* good excuses for failing to share our faith, *ever.* These excuses all emanate from "human concerns" (e.g., "I'm afraid," "I'm too busy," or "I'm an introvert"), no matter how spiritual they sound. They are attempts to justify disobedience. Blocking God's redemptive work—whether it's Peter trying to stop Jesus from dying on the cross or you refusing to let God speak through you to reach your lost friends—is exactly what Satan wants.

The game changer occurs when we realize that our rationalizations are nothing more than spiritual-sounding lies—in that moment, if we let it, apocalyptic urgency will roar through us like a tsunami.

The reality is that you *are* rcsponsible.

You *are* on the hook.

You have *skin* in this game.

There are *no* excuses.

If you don't share your faith, people *will* go to hell.

And it won't be God's fault.

God has done His work in Christ.

The fault will be yours, at least partially.

CHRIST'S AMBASSADORS

My fear at this point is that you're concerned I'm going to go all crazy on you. Maybe you think I'm going to ask you to put on a rainbow-colored wig and hold up John 3:16 posters at your local high school football game. I might do that, but only because I think it would be hysterical to play that kind of practical joke on you.

No, I believe the key to understanding how God might want you to go about reconciling friends and family members to Himself is found in Paul's use of the term *ambassador* (2 Cor. 5:20).

Ambassadors in Paul's time were people sent to foreign countries to speak on behalf of their king. Their responsibilities were identical to what they are today:

- Move to a foreign country.
- Learn the language.
- Respect the people and culture.
- Don't say or do anything that reflects poorly on the king.
- Communicate the king's message to foreign dignitaries.
- Press for a decision.
- Don't burn any bridges.

As Christ's ambassadors to nonbelievers within our circles of influence, that list pretty much sums up our part in the evangelism process. Our job is to build authentic relationships by learning their language (both literally and culturally), showing respect, being mindful of how our actions reflect upon Christ's cause, and when the opportunity presents itself, speaking "as though God were making his appeal through us" (2 Cor. 5:20).

Being an ambassador, however, is more than just presenting information. Ambassadors aren't sent to foreign countries because the sending country likes to keep other countries updated on their affairs. Matters of crucial importance are at stake, and decisions that affect national security must be made. Ambassadors deliver information and then call for a decision.

The reason you can't make excuses about not evangelizing is because you are needed to press for this decision! Jesus didn't say, "Go ye therefore and build religious billboards" or "Go ye therefore and hide evangelism tracts in public restrooms so when people have to relieve themselves they'll find out about me." He said, "You will be my witnesses" (Acts 1:8). That means we're called to make human to human contact. What your nonbelieving friends need is a Christian they trust who will clear his or her throat, look them in the eyes, explain the story of Jesus, and then ask them if they're ready to reconcile with God.

Paul wrote, "We implore you on Christ's behalf: Be reconciled to God" (2 Cor. 5:20). That's why God needs you. You may be the only ambassador of Jesus your nonbelieving friends will ever encounter. Do you understand that?

The issue is not *whether or not* you are Christ's ambassador to them—*you are*. God already decided that. The question is whether or not you are a good ambassador. Make all the excuses you want, God sent you into your circle of influence to do a job, and there is no plan B if you don't complete the job.

Jesus isn't going to send in the angels if you drop the ball. God isn't going to speak audibly to your friends to give them the opportunity to respond in faith to what He did in Jesus. Information about how to become a Christian will not spontaneously appear in your coworker's brain by the power of the Holy Spirit. The heavens aren't going to open up. The saints of old aren't going to come rushing in at the last second.

For whatever reason, God in His infinite wisdom (or audacity) chose to work through us to complete His ministry of reconciliation. What that means is you're the only plan God has.

You are the ministry of reconciliation.

Let that sink in.

You're it.

You're responsible.

Your coworker across the hall who trusts you—she's your responsibility. In order to reach your neighbor, the one who has never been to church in his life, God is looking to you. Apocalyptic urgency starts when we grasp the full implication of what this means. God has done His part, and has now passed to us the responsibility to reach every single person in our circles of influence. As the great missionary Robert E. Speer once wrote,

> Jesus Christ alone can save the world, but even Jesus Christ cannot save the world alone. He has no feet with which to go to the world but human feet, no lips with which to speak to the world but human lips, no eyes with which to look out upon the world but human eyes. The abounding needs of the world can only be met by the abounding sufficiency of Christ as men and women offer themselves as the channels of His grace to the world that is waiting for the light that it is to bring.[2]

But evangelism isn't just about responsibility, though that's a large part of it. The ministry of reconciliation is also a tremendous privilege.

In 2 Corinthians 5:17, Paul wrote, "If anyone is in Christ, the new creation has come." In the English translation, you miss the force of the original Greek. This phrase literally reads, "If anyone is in Christ, new creation!" There is no verb; it's just a noun and an adjective, and it's written as if it's a loud proclamation: *"New Creation!"* You can sense a feeling of awe even in Paul's simple phrasing.

Every time we help someone walk across the line of faith, we get a front-row seat to watch an astonishing act of creation. But unlike the acts of creation detailed in the book of Genesis, this creation happens in the heart, unseen by human eyes. But it's just as miraculous nonetheless.

That's why evangelism is a privilege. It's not just a *have to*, but a *get to*. Can you believe that God in His gracious compassion, given all that we put Him through because of our sin, turns around and allows us to participate in His effort to reclaim human lives? It's a stupendous act of grace. Who are we, creatures deserving God's full wrath because of our wickedness, to deserve such a privilege? It's astonishing to consider. The God of the universe not only refuses to count our sin against us, but also picks us up, brushes us off, looks us in the eye, and tells us that He *needs* us.

We're *needed?* What an honor!

FRONT-ROW SEAT

My church thought I was nuts. Out of the blue, I jumped into our church's baptistery with my clothes on in the middle of the worship service.

Other than my staff, no one, including my own family, had any idea what was going on. My wife later told me that as I did it, she was thinking to herself, *What in the world is he doing?* She was sitting next to my kids, and later told me they kept saying under their breath, "Oh my gosh. This is so embarrassing!"

Admittedly, it was the most bizarre, utterly random thing I had ever done in our church's ten-year history. No one in the auditorium knew what was going on. Everyone sat there with shocked looks on their faces.

Our church baptizes older children and adults by immersion, and for logistical reasons we schedule a baptism service once a month. However, we always communicate that our preference is that people get baptized immediately after making a confession of faith. Nevertheless, holding a standing monthly service is something that works for our church culture.

One day I had an idea. Call it what you will—inspiration, insanity, whatever. I started hearing excuse after excuse from my nonbelieving friends attending our church as to why they weren't ready to place their faith and trust in Christ. Eventually I became so frustrated with their excuses that one Sunday in the middle of the worship service I stopped my sermon, called our worship pastor and band to come back out on stage, and told the people in the room that the time for making excuses was over.

"This is a holy moment," I told everyone. "The Creator of the universe crossed heaven and earth to make it possible for you to spend eternity with Him after you die, and He's offering His forgiveness to you right now."

The band began playing in the background.

"No more excuses!" I repeated over and over again. I had been preaching on the parable of the lost sheep—the story of the shepherd who leaves the ninety-nine sheep in the open country to go look for that one lost sheep.

"That's you," I said. "Ever since you veered off on your own path, God has been worried sick over you like a parent that's lost a child! He's never stopped looking for you. He's never turned His attention away from reaching you, not for one second. From the moment you left His arms, He's turned over heaven and earth to bring you back."

Then I told everyone that we were going to give them an opportunity to make the decision to become a Christ follower, and right then, just like in the book of Acts, get baptized.

Now, just in case you're thinking, *That's nothing. We do that every week*—remember, I'm in predominantly Catholic, suburban Philadelphia. This doesn't happen, like, ever, in the churches in our region, which is part of the reason we schedule our baptism services once a month. But we hadn't scheduled one on this day.

"I know you might be scared," I continued. "I know many of you think that God can't forgive you for things you've done. I know you are concerned about what your friends and family will think. But today's the day when we're not going to make excuses. No more excuses."

Then I folded up my sermon notes, pushed my podium to the side, and walked to the edge of the stage.

"I'm going to do something we've never done in the history of our church. I'm going to jump into the baptistery with my clothes on. And I want you to join me. That's right. If you're ready, I want you to join me, in your clothes, right now."

Then I walked off the stage, went around the corner, and walked into the baptistery. And at first nobody came forward. *Nobody.*

Okay, this is going to get embarrassing, I thought.

Then one person came forward.

Then another person.

Then another.

And another.

Pretty soon a line of people wrapped around the corner of the hall leading to the baptistery. I couldn't believe it. I was shocked.

Again, let me stress, this was totally out of character for our church.

Wives brought up husbands. Parents came up with children. People who came to our church that day for the first time came forward. Every time someone came up from the water our congregation stood up and cheered like someone had scored a touchdown at a football game. It was absolutely amazing.

Each time I looked up, I saw another person make a decision to walk out of the crowd toward the baptistery. After people got baptized, others ran up to them and hugged them in their drenched clothing. The miraculous power of God's Spirit hung in the air while people sang, clapped, and made decisions to follow Christ. I had never been a part of anything like it before in my life.

Forty-four people came forward that day.

People have asked me since, "What was the best part of that experience for you?" And I tell them, "That's easy—watching people baptize their family members and friends."

My friend baptized his two teenage kids.

Wives baptized husbands.

Friends baptized friends.

Neighbors ran up and baptized neighbors.

One after another, people made commitments to Christ, repented of their sins, and got baptized on the spot by those who had been Christ's ambassadors in their lives, just like we read about in the book of Acts. My heart was overcome with awe as I watched person after person see the results of all of their time and effort invested in trying to reconcile lost friends and family members to God.

The tears. The smiles. The embraces of so many. All I could think about was how privileged we were to partner with God in this incredible act of redemption.

ONE FINAL REQUEST

I have just one more question I'd like to ask you: Do you believe any of this?

Be honest.

I've done my best to lay out for you why Jesus had to die, why hell makes sense in the larger story of the Bible, and how God has asked you to help Him bring nonbelievers into a saving relationship with Christ.

But do you believe it?

I ask you this because in the next chapter I'm going to begin to share practical ways you can reach out to your friends and family. My hope and prayer is that as a result of what I've already shared and the practical tools in the coming chapters, you'll lead a number of your friends to Christ.

But none of that will matter if you don't believe in hell.

Without 100 percent certainty in your heart that what the Bible says is actually true, you might convince a few friends to go with you to church, but that's about it. You will be no more effective for the kingdom than I was during the four years I was a pastor and didn't truly believe in hell.

So if I'm describing you, I have one last thing I'd like to ask you to do. Do this one thing, and then move on to the next chapter. If you're not willing to do what I'm about to ask of you, toss this book aside and stop reading, because the rest of the book won't help you anyway.

I want to ask you to repent.

I want to ask you to get down on the ground—literally, get face-down on the ground, completely prostrate—and tell God that you need Him to do something to your heart. I'm being serious.

Lie facedown on the ground as an act of repentance.

Tell God that you need a miracle.

Tell Him that you need to feel something.

My favorite passage when I was in this exact predicament was Mark 9:24: "I do believe; help me overcome my unbelief!"

Pray that prayer.

Over.

And over.

And over.

"I do believe; help me overcome my unbelief!"

Pray that until something happens in your heart.

Then repent of your arrogance. Repent of the sin in your life. Repent of the way you've allowed the "deceitfulness of wealth and the desires for other things [to] come in and choke the word, making it unfruitful" (Mark 4:19).

Repent of caring more about what non-Christian friends and family members think of you than about what God says is going to happen when they die. Repent of allowing important things in the kingdom, even vitally important causes, to overshadow your main purpose here on earth.

Stay on the ground, facedown, and ask God to help you see the world as He sees it. Ask Him to give you His heart for your coworkers, friends, relatives, and even enemies. Ask Him to help you literally feel what He feels when He locks eyes with those people. Ask Him to help you feel "great sorrow and unceasing anguish" in your heart (Rom. 9:2). Ask Him to allow you to be overcome with the same emotions Jesus felt as He carried His cross to a hill outside Jerusalem.

Ask Him to remove whatever sin, attitude, or memory that causes you to doubt.

Tell God that you repent of your laziness.

Tell Him that you repent of your cowardice. Repent if you think it's ridiculous that I would ask you to repent.

Listen, you can't think your way out of a faith crisis—I tried. I know this for a fact. I spent four years trying to conceptualize the idea of hell in a way that made sense to me, without realizing that this was a futile effort. "'For my thoughts are not your thoughts, neither are your ways my ways,' declares the LORD" (Isa. 55:8).

You can't *think* your way out of a faith crisis; you have to *repent* your way out of a faith crisis. The day I went to the monastery and spent almost an hour on the floor crying out to God, I got up a changed man, not because I began to think, but because I began to submit.

I'm praying that this happens to you.

I'm praying that God changes your heart.

I'm praying that God helps you in your unbelief.

Because whether you believe it or not, your non-Christian friends need you now more than ever.

NOTES

1. Carl F. H. Henry, quoted in "Mission Resources," *YWAMOrlando,* 2007, http://www.ywamorlando.com/contactus.asp.

2. Robert E. Speer, "The Abounding Sufficiency of Jesus Christ to Meet the Needs of All Men," in *Students and the Present Missionary Crisis,* (New York: Student Volunteer Movement for Foreign Missions, 1910), 12.

PART FOUR

IF HELL IS REAL ... HOW CAN I HELP OTHERS AVOID IT?

9
INTERESTED

There can be no doubt that as a matter of fact a religious life, exclusively pursued, does tend to make the person exceptional and eccentric.

—*William James*[1]

I am the world's worst handyman.

I don't mean that I'm an average handyman, or even a bad one. I wouldn't even call myself a *really* bad handyman. I am literally the worst handyman ever. In fact, if someone posted video clips of my attempts at basic household repair on YouTube, I promise you I would become an overnight Internet sensation—*that's how bad I am.*

I realized this the day Lisa and I moved into our first house and our furnace's pilot light went out. Somehow I convinced myself that the house was going to blow up, so I did something I quickly learned you're not supposed to do: I frantically called 911. Evidently firemen don't like to send out hook and ladder fire trucks, ambulances, and police cars at 1:42 a.m. just to help you relight your pilot light. Apparently new neighbors don't like it when you do that either.

Adding to the case against my ever receiving the "Mr. Home Improvement of the Year Award," large brown spots appear in my front yard every summer, but the lawn isn't my greatest challenge—it's the soaring weeds growing in the beds around the house. I've tried killing them, but I'm convinced they have some kind of supernatural death-resistant DNA, so I simply gave up trying. This past summer Lisa attempted to pull the weeds herself. She walked into the house forty-five minutes later covered in a thick layer of sweat and dirt and asked, "Where's the ax?"

It's not that I don't know we have two shutters that need to be rehung from the recent windstorm or a toilet seat in the downstairs bathroom that needs to be reattached or cars that haven't been waxed in years. I have a good friend who says that whenever he gets stressed, he spontaneously starts fixing and cleaning everything in sight. As a result, his house, lawn, and cars remain in pristine condition. Like a maintenance man turned personal trainer, my friend graciously reminds me of all the things I need to do on a regular basis. I, in turn, remind him that there has to be a perfectly safe medication on the market for whatever is ailing him.

Last year, to the shock of everyone who knows me, I singlehandedly bought, transported to my house, and replaced a toilet for our bathroom, and no one was significantly injured. My problem isn't that I'm not smart enough to do everything that's on my household to-do list. I'm pretty sure I can figure most of this stuff out. My problem isn't even time. I've got a few extra hours every week to squeeze some projects into my schedule.

My problem isn't any of these things.

My problem is simple: I'm the world's worst handyman because ever since that day on the monastery floor when God shook my heart like a ragdoll and shoved it full of apocalyptic urgency, all I've done is focus on reaching people far from God. That's it. Outside of my family, which I've always prioritized, that's all I've done. Anything beyond that priority, including handyman jobs around the house, falls by the wayside.

A few days after my monastery experience, I stumbled upon a passage of Scripture that became a life verse for me. Let me share it with you,

> What I mean, brothers and sisters, is that the time is short. From now on those who have wives should live as if they do not; those who mourn, as if they did not; those who are happy, as if they were not; those who buy something, as if it were not theirs to keep; those who use the things of the world, as if not engrossed in them. For this world in its present form is passing away. (1 Cor. 7:29–31)

Unlike the countless times I flipped open a Bible, read a passage, and closed the book no different from when I opened it, this time something reached out and grabbed me. I read that Scripture passage and I believed it. I began to believe that time was short. I believed that this world in its present form is passing away. Most important, I started looking at non-Christians as never before.

Now I don't care about having the best lawn in the neighborhood. That isn't even on my radar. Not even close. I don't care that there's a strange odor in my ten-year-old car that has a bazillion miles on it. I don't care that people my age with similar educations take more elaborate vacations, dress in much nicer clothes, spend countless hours analyzing investment portfolios embarrassingly larger than mine, and spend hours at the gym trying to obtain flawlessly trimmed midsections.

The reality is I couldn't care less about any of this because I've been assaulted by the belief that good people—friends, family members, fishing buddies, and T-ball coaches—kind, patriotic, spiritual, neighborly folks we picnic with and chat with are headed toward unrelenting torture in hell. The day I decided to believe this, my life (and my lawn) have never been the same.

I share this for one good reason: This is a stupid way to live your life. And it's a *horrible* way to try to make an evangelistic difference in the lives of your non-Christian friends.

That's right.

Don't do what I did. Don't do it.

It was a mistake.

Focusing all of my time and energy on leading a church to reach people far from God, and then throwing myself into personal evangelism to the exclusion of all other interests, was without question one of the biggest evangelistic blunders of my life.

NEED FOR BALANCE

Now I'm sure you're thinking to yourself, *I don't get it. This guy just spent the last eight chapters trying to help me come to grips with the reality of hell and my responsibility to reach my friends with the saving message of Christ; I thought for sure he was going to tell me to throw myself exclusively into personal evangelism.*

Not in the least.

Sure, I can look back on the last fifteen years and see the almost two thousand people God brought to faith in Christ directly or indirectly through my bumbling and feeble efforts. The new church I was starting at the time of my monastery experience went on to see hundreds of people come to faith in Christ. Then we moved to the suburbs of Philadelphia to start Christ's Church of the Valley, and seven of our neighbors started coming to our new church. In fact, in the first ten years alone we saw over a thousand people come to faith in Christ, many through personal efforts at evangelism.

God has enabled hundreds of these new Christians, with lives changed and marriages restored, to reach their family members and friends as well.

I absolutely threw myself into evangelizing people far from God. But I was misguided. I was wrong to go completely overboard with such a single-minded focus, and I regret my choice to live this way for two very simple reasons.

First, I misinterpreted 1 Corinthians 7:29–31. The last thing Paul is saying in this verse is to do what I did. What I realize now (but didn't realize years ago) is that Paul's exhortation in 1 Corinthians 7:29–31 was an example of ancient Semitic *overstatement.* It was a teaching technique. Oftentimes Jewish teachers would overstate a truth in such a way that underscored the importance of what was being said.[2] For example, Jesus Himself used the technique of overstatement in Matthew 10:34–36,

> Do not suppose that I have come to bring peace to the earth. I did not come to bring peace, but a

> sword. For I have come to turn "a man against his father, a daughter against her mother, a daughter-in-law against her mother-in-law—a man's enemies will be the members of his own household."

Jesus was not saying that we should hate our parents or children any more than Paul was saying that those of us who are married should ignore our spouses (i.e., "From now on those who [are married] should live as if they were not"). Paul's point in 1 Corinthians 7:29–31 is that Christ followers need to live with apocalyptic urgency because time is short, but that doesn't mean that we should ignore everything else in our lives. That's all he was trying to say. He just overstated his point. In fact, Paul's teaching elsewhere makes it abundantly clear that he believed living balanced lives and modeling healthy family relationships are key parts of making God's Word attractive to those outside the faith (Titus 2:10).

I was wrong to live with such a single-minded evangelistic focus for a second reason: I truly believe I would have been *twice* as effective evangelistically if I had lived a more balanced life. Let me make this clear—I *never* neglected my family. They have always been a priority for me. But after my monastery experience, I never made room for anything else besides my family, our church, and personal evangelism.

I look back over the last decade and a half and think about all the conversations I could have had with the neighbors if I had spent more time working in the yard. I wonder about how intense I seemed to people with whom I built relationships. I wonder how my lack of hobbies and attention to my own fitness, in addition to my constant feelings of being rushed and stressed, came across to the people I wanted to influence for Christ.

I truly believe if I had cultivated a more balanced life—including interests outside of just doing my job, loving my family, and trying to lead people to faith—more people would have come to faith in Christ, *not fewer*.

And I believe the same will be true for you.

GETTING PRACTICAL

We've spent a great deal of time wrapping our minds around why hell exists, why people stop believing in it, and what creates (or, in my case, recreates) urgency to help our friends and family avoid going there.

Granted, it was pretty theological at times, so I appreciate you hanging in with me thus far. Now it's time to get practical.

In the remaining chapters I want to help you translate what we've been talking about into action. I want to help you reach those within your circle of influence with the saving message of Christ. It's one thing to know the truth about hell. It's a completely different thing to help people avoid it. The challenge is learning to do evangelism in the context of our normal, everyday lives and responsibilities, not at the expense of them. Too often Christians have confused believing in hell, or telling non-Christians about it, with actual evangelism. Simply telling someone they're going to hell isn't evangelism. Many Christians are really good at that. The art of evangelism is helping people *want* to avoid hell.

My plan of action from here on out is to focus on five simple action steps you can put into place as soon as you put this book down.

That's it. *Just five simple ideas*. My experience with evangelism training is that it's often too complex. I've taught classes where I've given out notebooks and lectured for days, and at the end, the notebooks either went into the trash or onto the class members' bookshelves. Either way, I'm sure everyone who attended forgot everything we talked about within a week. The last thing you need from me is a series of detailed plans and strategies you'll never implement.

My goal is to stick a few ideas in your head that will provide a framework around which your natural gifts and personality can create a unique strategy for each person you meet.

WHAT MAKES YOU INTERESTING?

A few years ago I realized that our staff needed advice on how to lead our church to grow from thirteen hundred regular attendees to over three thousand. To provide some context, let me share our staff's philosophy of ministry. Our team is committed to leading our church to grow through conversion growth, not simply by doing things to encourage Christians attending other churches to transfer to ours.

In fact, growing through conversion is so important to us, I'm one of the only pastors I know who stands up on Christmas, Easter, and other high-attendance days of the year and *uninvites* churched visitors, just to make sure Christians in our area stay at their own churches and make them better.

"If you already attend a Bible-teaching church," I tell them, "please don't come back. This church isn't for you."

Our goal has never been, nor will it ever be, to build a church made up of Christians gathered from other churches. We're focused like a laser on conversion growth only.

Unsure of how to accomplish this bold objective of more than doubling the number of converts at our church, I turned to seasoned pastor Dr. E. LeRoy Lawson to come in and coach our staff. LeRoy was the senior pastor for years at a rapidly growing church in Mesa, Arizona, and I knew he had the wisdom and experience needed to help us chart the right course.

The day LeRoy arrived, I was taken aback by the first few words out of his mouth.

"You know, your pastor invited me to talk to you about how you can lead your church to grow from thirteen hundred to three thousand. I don't know how much help I'll be. I don't think you can manufacture such things, even if you tried. Instead, what I'd like to do is help you think about how to become the kinds of leaders three thousand new converts would want to follow."

Everyone on our staff leaned forward. We were hooked.

"What makes you interesting?" he asked.

Silence.

"Think about that for a moment," he said. "Most Christians are incredibly boring, wouldn't you agree?" Everyone nodded.

"I want to tell you about a friend of mine named Maud L. Eastwood. Maud is a worldwide doorknob expert. One day Maud invited me over to her house and showed me her vast collection of doorknobs. I honestly had no idea people collected such things, but Maud is a world-class expert. She's written books. She speaks at conventions. She travels around the world teaching seminars on doorknobs. Google her name when you get a chance."

Where's he going with this? I thought to myself. *And what does this have to do with evangelism and making converts?*

"It sounds crazy," he continued, "but I could sit and listen to Maud talk for hours on end about doorknobs. Why do you think that is? I think it's because, like all great teachers in school, she's interesting. I love listening to Maud talk about doorknobs. But here's the more important question: *Why* is Maud so interesting? I mean we're talking doorknobs for crying out loud! That has to be the most boring subject in the world to talk about. But Maud is captivating. Why? She's *interesting* because she's *interested*. Maud is head over heels *interested* in doorknobs. Why? Doesn't matter. She just is. And because she's interested, she's an interesting person to be around."

Lightbulbs went on all across the room, especially right over my head.

"I personally believe that those most effective at personal evangelism are those who are wildly interested in things that have absolutely nothing to do with their Christian faith. So, let me ask you again—what makes you interesting? If you really want to be effective evangelistically, the most important piece of advice I can give you is to develop a few interests in your life that when other people find out about them they tilt their head and say, 'No kidding?!'"

Then, just to make sure we knew that he practiced what he preached, Leroy went on to tell us about how he still continues to ride a Harley and water ski, even into his late seventies.

"Want to know why I ride a Harley and water ski? I originally started because I was interested in those things. I don't know how I got interested, doesn't matter. All that really matters is that those things have given me countless opportunities over the years to strike up conversations with people far from God. I wouldn't have been nearly as effective without them. Let's be honest, it's hard to relate to someone who talks all the time about God if you don't talk about God all the time yourself. Anyone can talk to someone who's interested in riding Harleys, especially if they're interested in motorcycles."

I was wrecked.

His words nailed me.

This was exactly what I needed to hear.

From this wise and seasoned older pastor, I learned what I now consider the first step to living with apocalyptic urgency and effectively sharing your faith: *Get interested.*

This principle is actually the very first thing Jesus taught His disciples when He called them to join Him in His audacious mission to help people find their way back to God.

> As Jesus was walking beside the Sea of Galilee, he saw two brothers, Simon called Peter and his brother Andrew. They were casting a net into the lake, for they were fishermen. "Come, follow me," Jesus said, "and I will send you out to fish for people." At once they left their nets and followed him. (Matt. 4:18–22)

We've all heard the phrase *fishers of men,* which we know is a creative play on words Jesus used to describe the main idea of evangelism to Simon and Andrew.

Here's my question—if we follow the logic of the metaphor a step further—what is the bait? If fishing for people means that Jesus' disciples help non-Christians become His followers, what do they use as bait?

Undoubtedly you've fished at least once in your life. Anyone who's ever been fishing knows that the concept is simple—you attach bait to a hook at the end of fishing line, which is attached to a fishing pole. When a fish takes the bait, you pull the pole back, tightening the line and lodging the hook in the fish's mouth. Then you reel the fish to shore. Pretty simple.

But what's the bait in Jesus' metaphor? If you haven't guessed yet, it's you and me. Christians are the bait. People wearing skin.

Every evangelism book, course, or training class I've ever gone through begins with teaching people "things to say" to non-Christians—as if we can find just the right words to entice non-believers to talk to us about coming to faith in Christ.

Listen, words aren't the bait.

You and I are the bait.

I've fished enough to know that if the fish aren't interested in what you put on the hook, you'll be grilling hamburgers when you get home. You will strike out and go home empty-handed. In the same way, if non-Christians aren't interested in *spending time* with you, there's no way they're going to be interested in what you have to say about God.

That's why the first step in effective evangelism is not memorizing Scripture or some prefabricated spiritual elevator speech. The first step is to go to work on yourself. Ask yourself whether or not you're the kind of person with whom a non-Christian would like to sit down and have a beer.

Many Christians will respond by saying, "No! That's absurd. The first step to effective evangelism is personal holiness—getting all your sins squared away." While I obviously think personal holiness is incredibly important for *maintaining* credibility with non-Christians, let's acknowledge that we both know lots of holy Christians whom non-Christians find incredibly strange. Just because you're committed to growing in Christ does not automatically make you an effective evangelist.

Evangelism begins when you get interested. If you want to reach your friends and help them avoid going to hell, here are two reasons why this is so important.

WHY GET INTERESTED?

1. Non-Christians Need to Be Able to Relate to You

There's a good chance that unless you're Amish, or my dad, you're on Facebook. I have thousands of "friends" on Facebook, and many of them are Christians. Because I use Facebook as a way to stay in touch with both Christians and non-Christians, it's interesting to observe the way other Christ followers communicate on Facebook. Here's what I've discovered: Many times when Christians write a "status" update, they channel their creepy inner TV evangelist. I don't get it. Surely these Christians have non-Christian "friends" who read this stuff.

For example, compare these status comments from two of my Facebook friends:

Jack wrote:

"The Spirit regenerates us so that our lifeless hearts can beat for God in a life of obedient worship of the one true God in Christ."

Perry wrote:

"They may be a bunch of 70-yr-old drag queens, but the Stones ROCK. Wanna know how a rock rhythm section should sound? 'Tumbling Dice' is exhibit A."

Jack's status update is obviously written by a Christian. No doubt many Christians might read that comment and find it encouraging. I'm not one of them, but there has to be some Christian who likes it, if for no other reason than it's just like many of the other Christian status updates on Facebook (along with either a Bible verse or an obscure Christian quote).

What about the second update from Perry? It's obviously a comment about the Rolling Stones. Obviously this guy knows the Stones' music because he's recommending a specific song. And I have no doubt that some Christians might not approve of listening to the Rolling Stones.

Would it surprise you to find out that the second status update is from an amazing professor at a Christian college? The man *loves* rock and roll music. He comments on it all the time. I check out his Facebook page whenever I'm online because he's so interesting. Honestly, I'm not that into classic rock (except for Lynyrd Skynyrd's "Free Bird"), but this guy is so interested in classic rock I can't help but be interested in it as well. He's like a walking encyclopedia—concert dates, band members, instruments used—there's no end to what this guy knows about 1970s and early '80s classic rock.

Which Christian do you think connects more with non-Christians? While it's obviously difficult to answer that based on one Facebook comment, my money is on Perry. Why? He's interesting. Why is he interesting? *He's interested.*

Non-Christians need something about you they can relate to, like a handle or relational lifeline of sorts. Since many people know nothing about the faith you feel so apocalyptically urgent about, there has to be something else about you they can relate to. It makes them feel comfortable, and in some strange way not judged by you.

I'm becoming friends with a non-Christian guy in our community. Whenever I see him, he walks right up to me and opens up a conversation. Want to guess what it's about? Jesus? Prayer? The Bible? Nope. *Soccer*. We've both spent time coaching soccer. Do I know anything about soccer? Not before I started coaching it. But I started as an assistant, went to coaching classes, and poured myself into learning everything I could about the sport. The result? Two years ago my team won the State Cup in our age group, no small feat. Did I coach because I like soccer? Not really. I've never played the sport in my life! I *became* interested in soccer, which then gave me something in common with dozens of other people like my non-Christian friend.

I worked for nine years with a *Star Wars* fan. Actually *fan* isn't the best word. *Star Wars* maniac is more like it. He's seen all the movies multiple times, memorizes *Star Wars* trivia, and networks with other *Star Wars* convention attendees. Yes, you heard me right. There are conventions all across the country where people dress up in *Star Wars* costumes and, well, I'm not sure what they do together, but my friend Frank knows. In fact, the theme for our summer Kids' Camp last year was "Kids' Camp Galaxy." Want to know what Frank did? He talked a dozen of his *Star Wars* friends into coming to our camp, dressed in their costumes. You should have seen the faces of the fourteen hundred children when they saw Darth Vader and the Stormtroopers standing at the door. Best part about that day? Not one of Frank's friends was a Christian.

I could go on and on.

How about you? What interests you?

Don't simply start a new hobby. Get interested in something so that you can share it with non-Christians in your circle of influence. What the Christian community lacks aren't fervent people, but fervently interesting people with whom non-Christians can connect. Effective evangelism doesn't begin complex strategies engineered to gain "face time" with nonbelievers; it starts with a genuine shared interest that creates a platform for friendship.

St. Irenaeus once wrote, "The glory of God is a living man."[3]

Living! Alive! Fully alive! Does that describe you? What brings you alive? What would you do if you had the time and felt encouraged by God to go pursue any activity? Surely there's something you've always wanted to do but never had the time or motivation to do it. Here's your chance! Do it. Throw yourself into it with reckless abandon for God's glory and the sake of the lost.

If you don't know what that one activity would be, experiment. Pursue something with reckless abandon. It may be something that other Christians consider strange, but who cares? There are plenty of non-Christians out there who won't care at all.

Find out what brings you great joy, and then go do that thing with as many non-Christians as you can befriend. That interest of yours will become the handle that allows people far from God to grab on to your life and connect to your heart.

2. Christians Need to Continually Reinvent Themselves for a Lifetime of Effectiveness

When I was in college, someone gave me a cheesy Christian T-shirt that read, "Live like you'll die tomorrow; die knowing you'll live forever."

Like Paul's words in 1 Corinthians 7:29–31, that's obviously an overstatement, because if it's not, it's a corny philosophy for living your life. If I truly believed I was going to die tomorrow, I'd skip work, eat enormous amounts of chocolate peanut butter ice cream, and do nothing but spend time with my family. I could do that for a day, but not two days, and definitely not three. The sugar buzz alone would put me into a coma.

The reality is that you can't live your life planning as if you will die tomorrow. You need to approach evangelism as if you're going to live a full life. In my opinion, apocalyptically urgent Christians should plan on serving God evangelistically until they're ninety-nine years old, not as if they're going to heaven tomorrow! If you do that, you'll cut out the kinds of interests in your life that will enable you to be a deep, mature, and interesting human being. You won't read books, mow the lawn, or pursue hobbies—all because you're trying to spend every available moment (as I did for years) sharing your faith.

The question we need to ask ourselves is, "How can God use me evangelistically throughout my *entire* life, not just in a short two- or three-year spurt?"

How many Christians do you know who *used* to evangelize? They can proudly point to a time in their lives when person after person came to Christ through their efforts, then for some reason they just stopped. (I can name fifty such people off the top of my head.)

My hunch is they stopped sharing their faith because they either stopped believing in hell or they got bored in life—possibly both. God wants us to lead people to faith in Christ until we take our last breaths. He wants us to be more effective today than yesterday, more effective this year than last, more effective in our sixties and seventies than we were in our twenties and thirties. At the very end of our lives we want to be able to say with the apostle Paul that we are "being poured out like a drink offering, and the time for [our] departure is near" (2 Tim. 4:6). We left no evangelistic opportunity wasted. No excuses. No regrets.

But in order to do that we have to stay fresh.

We have to stay interested.

To keep fresh personally, a few years ago I started what I call my very own "MA Program." Since many MA degrees are completed in a year, I started this hobby where I study something completely foreign to me for an entire year.

The first year I studied country music. To the absolute shock of everyone who knew me, I made myself leave the radio locked on the country station for one entire year. And man it was tough, at least initially. The good news is that I survived, and gained a little twang in my singing voice.

Why do that? One reason is that I've always wanted to fully understand and appreciate a genre of music with which I had no experience. The other reason is that I wanted to be able to have conversations with people who listen to 92.5 WXTU, a popular country station in our area. Now I'm familiar with artists like Keith Urban and Kenny Chesney. I know what the CMT awards are. And I'd like to take a trip to Nashville at some point. Best of all, if you're a country-music-listening-cowboy-boot-wearing non-Christian, I'm ready for you. I would type "Yee Haw" right now, but that would be a little freaky.

One year for my own personal MA program I studied European history and geography, and then Lisa and I took a trip for our twentieth anniversary to visit the museums and major cultural sites of Italy, Switzerland, France, and England. Another year for my MA program I studied Greek history and mythology. God willing, at some point in my life when I can afford it, I'm going to "finish" the course by taking a trip with Lisa to tour Greece and its beautiful islands.

One year I studied Native American history. We all know the tragic story, but I wanted to understand what happened—the key figures, geography, culture, and political factors. After a year of study, our family spent some time in the Black Hills on the way back from a Yellowstone vacation. Hiking the land stolen from the Lakota people had a profound impact on me. I've never talked with Native American friends the same way after that year.

I go through all this trouble each year for one reason: I believe my best evangelistic years are ahead of me. I truly believe that God is going to strategically place people in my life that will need me ten, twenty, thirty, and hopefully forty years from now, *and I want to be ready*. Years from now I believe I could have a conversation where something I learned in one of my MA programs will come up in conversation, and a nonbeliever will tilt his head and say, "No kidding. I thought I was the only one interested in these kinds of things." You never know.

In the meantime, I'm staying fresh. I'm staying interested. I'm trying to be the kind of person that a non-Christian would have a beer with, even though I don't drink. In light of this, I believe staying interested is one of the most important evangelistic activities in which I can engage.

My next MA program is sitting in my garage. My friend let me borrow his telescope, and this telescope isn't the kind you get your kid for Christmas. It's literally five feet high, a full eighteen inches thick, and looks like a missile getting ready to launch. Since I was seven years old and accidentally found the rings of Saturn in my childhood telescope, I've been interested in astronomy. So next year I'm making time to throw myself into reading astronomy books, stargazing in the backyard, and attending stargazing events so I can start up conversations with professional astronomers in our area. I may even take a class at our local college.

The only thing I do know is that if I'm interested, there's a good chance I'm going to cross paths with a non-Christian who's interested in astronomy as well.

As long as he's not into basic household repair, I think we'll get along just fine.

NOTES

1. William James, *The Varieties of Religious Experience*, Centenary Edition (New York: Routledge, 2002), 11.

2. See R. H. Stein, *The Method and Message of Jesus' Teachings* (Philadelphia: The Westminster Press, 1978), 8.

3. St. Irenaeus, *Against Heresies*, 4.20.7, eds. Alexander Roberts and James Donaldson, *Ante-Nicene Fathers* (Peabody, MA: Hendrickson,1999), 1:490.

10

CHILL

We do not want churches because they will teach us to quarrel about God, as the Catholics and Protestants do. We do not want to learn that. We may quarrel with men sometimes about things on this earth. But we never quarrel about God. We do not want to learn that.

—*Chief Joseph of the Nez Perce*[1]

A few months after I gave my life to Christ, at the age of eighteen, I flew out to Arizona to spend some time with my older sister and her boyfriend, who happened to be Jewish. I knew they were dating seriously and were talking about marriage, so I viewed this opportunity as a divinely appointed moment to convert him.

The first night, after a delightful evening meal at their favorite Mexican restaurant, we went back to the house and watched basketball. Midway through the fourth quarter I realized it was getting late, and since I didn't have long to spend with them, I awkwardly leaned over and told him that I'd love to talk to him about his religious beliefs.

He told me he was Jewish, and I told him he was going to hell.

Then we argued for six straight hours.

We fought (or more accurately, I fought with him) from ten o'clock that night until four o'clock the next morning. It got so bad that around two o'clock we got into the car and drove around for a few hours, meandering through the streets of Tucson as I volleyed argument after argument at him about why he needed to become a Christian.

Then at four in the morning, right in the middle of all of my seemingly airtight arguments for the deity of Jesus, the infallibility of the Bible, and the reality of hell, he asked me a simple question.

"Brian, if what you believe is true, why do you treat your sister so poorly?"

"What do you mean?" I sheepishly asked, as a lump slowly formed in my throat.

"You never call her," he said. "You're always in a rush. I mean she flies you out to spend the weekend with her, and you've been fighting with me for the last six out of the nine hours you've been here. Brian, I don't know much about Christianity, but if what you're saying is true, then I would have thought that I'd see a change in the way you treat her."

He was absolutely right.

I was an idiot—a well-meaning, misguided idiot—but an idiot nonetheless. And rather than spending time with my sister, I unleashed my "shock and awe" evangelistic barrage on my future brother-in-law. And all of this came from someone who had been a Christian for a total of two months.

"You're right," I said. "I'm sorry."

On the way back to my sister's apartment, I sat in the passenger's seat, silently reeling from the emotional aftermath of my six-hour tirade. Then a random thought occurred to me—I didn't even know his parents' names. I never once asked him a question about his business. I didn't know about his plans for the future. Not once did I ask him about his relationship with my sister, their plans for having children, or what he liked to do in his spare time.

I didn't know any of that about him, yet I presumed I could fly in, dump a load of Jesus talk on him, and expect him to change the twenty-six-year trajectory of his entire life after one discussion with me.

If I had just shut up and listened, I would have discovered that he was an amazing, caring, and funny person. But I didn't. I came on conversationally as if the Hoover Dam had exploded.

If I had taken the time over that weekend to learn a couple of things about someone my sister obviously cared about, then maybe a year or two later God might have opened a door for me to have a serious conversation with him about his faith. By that time, maybe I would have gained enough credibility with him that he would have opened up to me.

But I didn't do that.

I felt as if I had completely burned that bridge.

By the grace of God, he did eventually come to faith, some twenty years later, but not as a result of my influence. He came to Christ *in spite of me*. And just to give you an indication of the kind of brother-in-law I have now, he's never brought that incident up. Not once.

At least one of us knows how to be Christlike.

PAUL'S EXAMPLE

Over the years I've taken solace in the fact that I'm not the only Christian to come on too strong evangelistically. The apostle Paul's actions in the first few months after he came to faith in Christ make my story pale in comparison.

While leaving town on a trip to hunt down Christians, the great persecutor of the church was struck down with blindness by the risen Jesus. Stunned and bewildered, Saul (who was also called Paul) was led into the city of Damascus where "for three days he was blind, and did not eat or drink anything" (Acts 9:9).

Meanwhile a Christian in Damascus named Ananias saw a vision of God, who instructed him to go to Saul and place hands on him to heal his blindness. God let Ananias know that "this man is my chosen instrument to proclaim my name to the Gentiles" (v. 15).

Reluctantly, Ananias obeyed and found Saul.

> Then Ananias went to the house and entered it. Placing his hands on Saul, he said, "Brother Saul, the Lord—Jesus, who appeared to you on the road as you were coming here—has sent me so that you may see again and be filled with the Holy Spirit." Immediately, something like scales fell from Saul's eyes, and he could see again. He got up and was baptized, and after taking some food, he regained his strength. (vv. 17–19)

What an amazing experience! Singled out, chosen to be Jesus' instrument to proclaim His forgiveness, cleansed of his sin—Paul could hardly contain himself.

So what did he do? Acts 9:20 tells us, "At once he began to preach in the synagogues that Jesus is the Son of God."

At once.

No hesitation.

The exact same approach I took with my future brother-in-law.

Paul's apocalyptic urgency consumed him, propelling him to reach out and try to save as many people as he possibly could. We're told that he "spent several days with the disciples in Damascus" (v. 19). What happened during that time as a result of his preaching?

For one we're told that he "grew more and more powerful and baffled the Jews living in Damascus by proving that Jesus is the Messiah" (v. 22).

That's impressive. I can't remember ever "baffling" anyone with the logic of my words. But that's not all.

"All those who heard him were astonished" (v. 21). Now that's really impressive. No one, as best as I can recall, has ever been astonished by my preaching.

But what did Paul have to show for his baffling and astonishing evangelistic efforts? Not a thing. Not a single person in Damascus converted.

If anything, Paul's time there had the opposite effect—the Jews tried to kill him.

> After many days had gone by, there was a conspiracy among the Jews to kill him, but Saul learned of their plan. Day and night they kept close watch on the city gates in order to kill him. But his followers took him by night and lowered him in a basket through an opening in the wall. (vv. 23–25)

After his narrow escape Paul made his way to Jerusalem, where he repeated the same Herculean effort at trying to convert people there. "When he came to Jerusalem … He talked and debated with the Hellenistic Jews" (vv. 26, 29).

And the result there? Once again "they tried to kill him" (v. 29).

Same behavior. Same results.

Fortunately the Christians in Jerusalem had enough foresight to see the potential in this apocalyptically urgent but misguided new Christ follower. They did what they could to keep him from getting himself killed.

"When the believers learned of this, they took him down to Caesarea and sent him off to Tarsus" (v. 30).

And then, in what has to be the most comical verse in the Bible, we are told, "Then the church throughout Judea, Galilee and Samaria enjoyed a time of peace" (v. 31).

The entire church in that region breathed a collective sigh of relief.

WHAT IT MEANS TO CHILL OUT

From Paul's story we learn another step to living with apocalyptic urgency and effectively sharing your faith: *Chill out.*

To me, chilling out evangelistically means three things.

1. Don't Come On Too Strong

Without question, one of the biggest mistakes Christians make when they realize hell is real is to immediately come on too strong.

You can understand how it happens. If one day you're married to a great non-Christian woman, and the next day you realize that she is an object of God's wrath, you would pull out the heavy artillery.

It's a natural response.

You drag her to church. You read up on evangelistic techniques. You turn on the Christian radio station when you're both in the car (even though most of the music on it is just horrible). It doesn't matter because you're desperate. Because of your love for her, you're suddenly willing to do whatever it takes to lead your wife across the line of faith, *like, yesterday*.

My advice? Stop it.

If you truly love your wife, or anyone who doesn't believe in Christ right now, take a deep breath, pause, collect your thoughts, and chill. This will undoubtedly be one of the most important things you will ever do to lead someone to faith. Trust me.

Chilling out means taking stock of your situation and making sure that you don't come across like a Jesus freak to those you are trying to reach. Doing so can turn someone off to Christianity for a long time, maybe even forever.

The apostle Paul wrote in Romans 12:11, "Never be lacking in zeal, but keep your spiritual fervor, serving the Lord." That verse appears to be saying the exact opposite of what I just encouraged you to do.

In his commentary on Romans, New Testament scholar Douglas Moo provides a much more literal translation of this verse from the Greek: "In zeal, do not be lazy. Be set on fire by the spirit; Serve the Lord."[2]

Catch that?

Paul is saying "Let God's Spirit burn inside you. Stay consumed. Keep your fervor high. Never lose your *passion* to reach those outside the family of God."

The reality is that verse is saying exactly what it appears to be saying. However, the problem is if you come on too strong, as I did, when you're sharing your faith, you're not keeping your fervor alive; you're just becoming obnoxious.

Zeal does not mean you act pushy. Some of the most apocalyptically urgent people I know are incredibly patient. As Proverbs 19:2 points out, "Desire without knowledge is not good—how much more will hasty feet miss the way!"

Let's say, for instance, you go out and buy a new Volkswagen Beetle, and over time you become convinced that no one will truly be happy until they own a Beetle. So you start telling every person you meet that he or she should own a Beetle.

You start forwarding emails about Beetles to your non-Beetle-owning friends. You start leaving little VW Beetle flyers around for people to read. You constantly say "I love Beetles" or type in quotes from the Beetle owner's manual as your Facebook status.

Whenever you talk with your friends, you always manage to slip the phrase "Praise Beetles" into the conversation. You may even buy a Beetle bumper sticker to put on the back of your Beetle, or a Beetle T-shirt to influence your non-Beetle-owning friends. You make it a point to only listen to Beetle-centric radio stations while driving, and watch Beetle-focused programs on television.

You start belittling people for not going to weekly Beetle meetings, and when something goes wrong in a non-Beetle-owner's life, you say things like, "That's because you don't own a Beetle."

Over time you get to the point where you are afraid to be around people who don't own Beetles because you might become corrupted, tempted by other cars. Eventually, as you might guess, you become so obnoxious that non-Beetle owners can't stand being around you.

What's the problem? Is your problem Volkswagen Beetles? Of course not.

But that's what many Christians do when apocalyptic urgency grips their hearts; they get weird for some reason. They start talking in a weird Christianese language they learn from TV evangelists or people on the radio. They start wearing stupid Christian T-shirts. They cut themselves off from the larger culture and grow narrow-minded. They do things that have everything to do with blinded social segregation and nothing to do with genuine Christian holiness. They just become strange.

That's why I think the second action step for anyone who wants to live out a life full of apocalyptic urgency is to simply chill out. Don't allow yourself to become a caricature of the prototypical pushy and obnoxious Christian.

2. Trust the Process of Evangelism

The second thing chilling out means is to *trust the process* of evangelism.

Effective personal evangelism is not an all-or-nothing, one-time, one-person, take-it-or-leave-it proposition; it's a process that involves lots of people working together over time to bring someone to faith in Christ.

Most Christians I know don't get this.

The other day I went to breakfast with another pastor I don't know very well. He was hoping for some good ideas that would help his church reach out to his community. When we ordered our meal, he told the waitress, to my utter shock, that he wanted to talk to her about what it means to have a relationship with Jesus Christ. I wanted to duct tape the menu over his mouth and shut him up.

Have you ever done this? Or have you ever been around Christians who have done this type of thing at the wrong place and the wrong time?

There's a church in our area that sends teams of people out on Monday nights to visit first-time guests (without an appointment) who visited on Sunday. They basically show up on their doorsteps and try to lead these people to Christ on the spot.

One of my staff members, an experienced pastor, visited this particular church while he was on vacation a few years back, just to see what their services were like. The next night five men showed up on his doorstep.

"Sir, we were wondering if we could come in and talk to you about what it means to have a relationship with Jesus Christ."

"Um, I'm one of the pastors at Christ's Church of the Valley."

"That's great," one of the men said. "But do you know if you're going to go to heaven after you die?"

"Like I said, I'm a pastor right down the street."

"Yes, but …" another person jumped in. "*Do you know for sure* you're going to heaven?"

If it wasn't so embarrassingly sad, it would be funny.

Most Christians come on too strong after they start believing in hell because they don't realize that evangelism is a process. Evangelism was never meant to be an all-or-nothing proposition; it's a team activity. We learn this from 1 Corinthians 3:5–7:

> What, after all, is Apollos? And what is Paul? Only servants, through whom you came to believe—as the Lord has assigned to each his task. I planted the seed, Apollos watered it, but God has been making it grow. So neither the one who plants nor the one who waters is anything, but only God, who makes things grow.

Paul is saying that the Christians in the church in Corinth couldn't point to just one person and say, "That person alone led me to Christ." Paul shared his faith. Another pastor named Apollos continued to teach the way of Jesus to those seeking to understand. Others had conversations that helped propel each person along in his or her journey. God grew that seed of faith in the hearts of seekers. But no one person brought anyone to faith alone.

In a previous chapter we talked about how you are responsible for sharing your faith with your nonbelieving friends in your sphere of influence. That doesn't mean you're responsible for converting them all by yourself, from start to finish. You may be the first person to talk to someone about Christ, or you may be the one who actually leads him or her across the line of faith, but in between there's usually a long string of faithful Christians who helped along the way.

Saying that evangelism is a process means two things.

First, many people will have a hand in leading a person to faith in Christ; conversion rarely happens because of just one conversation.

Second, your goal in evangelism is to *remove barriers* keeping someone from trusting in Christ, not to sit down, have one conversation, and take a complete non-Christian across the line of faith all at once.

Think of the barriers that exist in the mind of a nonbeliever as he or she considers the prospect of becoming a Christian. The average non-Christian I know struggles with the idea of believing in God, let alone Jesus, so that's a huge barrier all by itself. If they are able to believe in God, then they move on to figuring out which God is the right one. If they get past that barrier, which most don't, they will struggle with the idea that the Bible is God's Word. Then there's the whole business of Jesus—who He is and what He claims to be.

Depending upon the person and his or her life experience, the list of barriers can be lengthy. So many barriers exist between where that person lives spiritually and making a commitment to Christ that it's ridiculous to think that someone might come to faith based on one conversation. Yes, it happens, but usually God has already been working in that person's heart long before.

Picture yourself stuck in downtown traffic and needing to get to the other side of town in a short period of time. Bumper-to-bumper traffic clogs the streets. You decide to take a side street to beat the traffic. Once you turn you see a series of concrete barriers in the middle of the street. Unable to turn around or lift the barriers yourself, you have to wait for someone from the city to remove the barriers one by one until the way is clear.

When you initiate a friendship with someone far from God, your job is to remove the barriers that stand between that person and God. Your job may be to remove that first barrier, or to remove the second one. In a rare instance, your job may be to remove many barriers over a long period of time, eventually helping this person cross the line of faith.

The point is that nonbelievers have lots of barriers that stand in the way of their making faith commitments, and they need time to process everything they hear along the way. You can't come on too strong, and you can't assume you're going to be the only one who will make a difference in that person's life.

Some Christians point to Jesus' command in Matthew 10:14 as the way Christians should share their faith: "If anyone will not welcome you or listen to your words, leave that home or town and shake the dust off your feet."

Shock and awe, baby! Give them both barrels.

If they don't respond, shake the dust off your feet and move on.

That's a great approach to evangelism if you are literally one of the twelve apostles and Jesus Himself shows up to give you the command to "go rather to the lost sheep of Israel" (Matt. 10:6). But until the Son of God Himself physically shows up and gives you that command, it's probably best to chill out. That Scripture verse is referring to a specific time during Jesus' life, and holds no relevance for evangelism today.

The pastor I had breakfast with—maybe his job that day was to let the waitress know that he was a Christian, tell her that she was doing a fabulous job, and give her a larger than usual tip. Maybe those simple actions would have removed an "all Christians are freaky" barrier in her mind. Instead, he probably erected a new barrier that another Christian is going to have to deal with someday.

When we hear about people coming to faith in Christ after just one conversation, ninety-nine times out of a hundred you'll find that the Christian who pressed for a decision wasn't the first believer to arrive on the scene. The fruit was already ripe. All he or she had to do was shake the tree a bit before it fell to the ground.

That's what I mean when I say that evangelism is a process—taking a nonbeliever closer to the cross and removing one barrier at a time.

3. Trust the One Who Controls the Process

At the core of scriptural evangelism is trust. Not just in the process of evangelism, but in the One who oversees the process of evangelism. Do I trust that God is going to do everything He can to lead someone across the line of faith, even if I'm not the one to do it?

Ultimately, it's about releasing control and trusting that God will raise up other people to work in the lives of our friends. It's about trusting God to work while the person with whom we're sharing takes the time needed to process all the information.

It took me eighteen years to put my faith and trust in Christ. That's a long time. There were lots of people along the line, endless conversations, lots of prayers, and immense anxiety in the hearts of those who loved me and wanted to see me become a Christian. But throughout it all, God was faithful.

My high-school baseball coach, Spencer Sindell, shared a great line before one of our playoff games. "Relaxed intensity," he told us. "That's what we need right now, men. Cool composure on the outside with a fiery intensity underneath."

I can't think of a better way to describe what I mean by chilling out.

On the one hand, we feel "great sorrow and unceasing anguish" in our hearts for our friends who are headed to hell after they die

(Rom. 9:2). On the other hand, we know that if we come on too strong, or push them to make a decision too quickly, we'll only erect more barriers.

That's why I love the way the ancient Roman emperor Marcus Aurelius described his friend Apollonius. In his famous work *Meditations*, Aurelius wrote about each of the aspects of his personal character that he learned from individuals in his life.

From his friend Apollonius he thankfully acknowledged learning,

> To see clearly in a living example that a man can be at once very much in earnest and yet able to relax.[3]

That's a description of relaxed intensity, otherwise known as chilling out. That's trusting that God is going to be faithful. That's what your nonbelieving friends need from you.

THE PROCESS IN ACTION

A few years ago I asked a friend of mine, a staunch atheist, to join me for lunch.

"Let's just catch up. No spiritual talk," I said.

"No problem," he said.

I decided to take him to Bob Evans. The great state of Ohio, where I was born, gave the world two beautiful gifts. The first is Ohio State Buckeye football, God's favorite college sports team. The second is Bob Evans, a southeastern Ohio based chain restaurant known for their "down on the farm" cooking. I figured that if I hit another spiritual brick wall with my friend, like I had in the past, at least I would enjoy a good meal at a good price.

Halfway through lunch, after we talked about some political issue, he put his fork down and asked me, "What do you think happens when we die?"

"I thought we weren't going to talk about religion," I responded.

"Well, I know what you're going to say, but it's been on my mind a lot lately."

"What do *you* think happens when we die?" I shot back.

He paused, pointed at my Wildfire Chicken Salad, and said, "Same thing that happens to that head of lettuce."

"You don't *really* believe that, do you? As if all of this—you, me, this planet, the universe—all of this is some cosmic accident and we're here all alone?"

"Absolutely I do."

"Well," I said, as I wiped my mouth with my napkin, "what exactly do you believe if you had to give your beliefs a name?"

"I'm more into a Hindu sort of approach to the world."

"Really? This coming from a guy who wouldn't recognize a Hindu belief if it ran him over on the freeway!"

"Jones, seriously. I like that Gandhi guy. I mean, I saw a special about him on TV the other day and I thought to myself, *Now he's got it all together. That's what I believe. I'm a follower of Gandhi.*"

"Gandhi?"

"Yep. Gandhi."

"Gandhi over Jesus?"

"Absolutely. I don't know what your deal is with Jesus is anyway. Don't know why he's any more special than any other great religious teacher, especially Gandhi."

"I can't believe I'm hearing this from the guy who covers himself head to toe in green paint and screams like a maniac at Eagles' football games. Gandhi?"

"Gandhi."

"Can I ask you a question?"

"Shoot."

"Do you even know anything about Gandhi? I hear atheists like you say all the time what a wonderful person Gandhi is. Do you even know anything about him?"

"What do you mean?"

"Gandhi did a lot of great things for his people, I'll give you that, but the last person you should hold up as a great moral example is Gandhi. Did you know that Gandhi used to practice something called *brahmacharya?* Any idea what that is?"

"Never heard of it."

"It's a spiritual practice where Hindu holy men sleep next to a naked woman to prove they have the self-restraint not to have sex with them. If they successfully spent the night with them without having intercourse, they proved to themselves, the woman, and the world they have heightened spiritual abilities and self-control."

Silence.

"Gandhi routinely practiced brahmacharya, but here's the kicker—he did it with underage women."

"Shut up."

"I'm serious."

"He did not!"

Then I shared with him what all scholars who have studied Gandhi's life know about him—Gandhi had a need, bordering on obsession, to practice strange brahmacharya experiments with teenage girls.

Elizabeth Abbott, former dean of women at Trinity College in Toronto, is just one of the many scholars who points out that Gandhi "requested that various young women—teenaged virgins or newlyweds—sleep next to him to warm him."[4]

Abbott points out that Abha, Gandhi's great-nephew's sixteen-year-old wife, "had to remove her clothes so Gandhi could judge whether he, like Ramananda [another Hindu holy man], was sufficiently chaste to be unaffected by her nakedness. Abha's husband was so distressed he offered himself in his wife's place; he, himself, would keep the old man warm at night. But no, Gandhi wanted Abha for his brahmacharya experiment."[5]

Abbott goes on to point out that "another teenager, distant cousin Manu Gandhi, bathed and shaved Gandhi, slept with him, monitored his physical condition during his fasts, and gave him enemas."[6]

"Did you know any of this?" I asked my Hindu-obsessed friend across the table.

"Had no idea."

"We have a name for that kind of behavior in this country; four words to be exact: corruption of a minor. I didn't bring this up to bash Gandhi; this is simply an established fact about his life. It's well-documented. I bring it up because you compared him to Jesus, and quite frankly, Gandhi isn't even in the same league as Jesus Christ. No one is, in fact. That's the point."

He just sat there silently. Didn't say a word. He just moved his fork around, playing with his food, and processed everything I had just shared. Somehow I sensed that God was working on his heart and a spiritual barrier had been removed. I think he realized it too.

So I did what any apocalyptically urgent person should do in this situation—I changed the subject. I said, "That's enough talk about religion for one day. How's your wife's job?"

You're probably thinking, *You had him against the ropes, why didn't you press for a decision? Why didn't you ask him what was preventing him from surrendering his life to Christ, right there, that instant?*

I didn't press him to make a decision because I knew that removing one barrier didn't mean I removed all his barriers. I couldn't allow my fear of losing my friend to hell to cause me to barge ahead.

The famous nineteenth-century atheist Bertrand Russell once observed, "Zeal is a bad mark for a cause. Nobody has any zeal about arithmetic. It is not the vaccinationists but the antivaccinationists who generate zeal. People are zealous for a cause when they are not quite positive that it is true."[7]

I think what Russell was getting at wasn't zeal, but overzealousness. And if that's what he meant, I would agree with him. I know Christianity is true. I know Jesus is far superior to Gandhi, or any other religious teacher this world has ever seen. But that doesn't give me the right to ride roughshod over a spiritual seeker's need to process the decision to come to faith in Christ for him or herself.

I did, however, leave what I call a "lifeline" at the end of our conversation, which is a simple action step I like to give people when I sense they're not yet ready to cross the line of faith. I asked my friend if he'd be willing to read a chapter in a book and get together at some future point to talk about it.

He agreed.

And that was it.

No miraculous conversion that day, just one tiny barrier removed.

Yet I had faithfully fulfilled my duty as a loving Christian.

The good news is that my friend eventually came to faith in Christ a few years later through the help of another good friend of mine.

The bad news is I got stuck with the check that day.

(Hey, I may not be pushy, but I am cheap.)

NOTES

1. Chief Joseph of the Nez Perce, quoted in Keny Nerburn, ed., *The Wisdom of the Native Americans* (Novato, CA: New World Library, 1999), 35.

2. Douglas J. Moo, *The Epistle to the Romans* (Grand Rapids, MI: Eerdmans, 1996), 778.

3. Marcus Aurelius, *The Meditations of The Emperor Marcus Antoninus*, trans. A. S. L. Farquharson (United States of America: Oxford University Press, 1944), 4.

4. Elizabeth Abbott, *A History of Celibacy* (New York: Scribner, 2000), 225.

5. Ibid.

6. Ibid.

7. Bertrand Russell, quoted in Madeleine L'Engle, *Walking on Water* (New York: North Point, 1995), 47.

11
RELATIONSHIPS

Christians are to *be* the good news before
they *share* the good news.
—*Joe Aldrich*[1]

In 1986 I went through a "casting demons out of people" phase. It was around this time I also went through a "I'm going to wear a mullet like Bono from U2" phase. For the life of me I can't decide which phase was more ridiculous.

As I mentioned in the previous chapter, soon after my eighteenth birthday I became a Christian. What I didn't mention is that my conversion was pretty dramatic. Within months I led a few dozen people to Christ and was feeling drawn to full-time Christian service. My dramatic conversion presented a problem—my newfound zealousness surpassed everyone around me, and the church where I grew up quickly became a chore to attend.

I'm not being fed here, I thought arrogantly. *These people just don't have what I need spiritually*. Fortunately, I soon discovered that there was a better spiritual alternative. A new church popped up on the southeast side of Columbus, led by a fanatical young TV pastor named Rod Parsley.

This guy's on fire, I thought as I watched him on TV. *I've got to go out there and be a part of that action!*

My friends and I jumped into my dad's Pontiac Bonneville and headed down the road to Parsley's World Harvest Church. When we walked into the service, we were in shock. The worship and singing part of the service alone lasted for over an hour. People danced in the aisles. Rod did this thing where he placed his handkerchief on people's foreheads and they'd fall over. *This guy has it going on*, we thought.

The best part was that he had the ability to cast demons out of people. Fortunately, he wanted the rest of us to learn how to do it as well. I was just lucky, I guess. If I hadn't stumbled upon Rod, I never would have learned how to eject a supernatural demonic being from a person's body.

Here's how Rod told us to do it:

Step One: *Place your hand on the possessed person's forehead and position your body in the Heisman Trophy stance.*

I'm not sure what it was about placing the hand on the forehead or the Heisman Trophy touchdown pose, but it worked for Rod every time. It didn't matter if the person was possessed by twenty demons; once Rod broke into the Heisman pose, we knew the demon was toast and we'd get to Denny's in time to beat the Baptists to lunch.

Step Two: *Yell directly at the demon, preferably in King James English.*

Evidently demons are hard of hearing, or easily intimidated, so always remember to speak *loudly* and always have a few handy phrases memorized from seventeenth-century English. "Depart, foul demon!" and "Returneth to thy hellish abode!" seemed to be a few phrases that always worked for Rod.

Step Three: *If you find the demon doesn't want to leave, shake the person's head back and forth.*

Apparently really tough demons only come out after intense physical shaking. That's understandable. I know I couldn't go about my business when there's a 7.0 earthquake on the Richter scale going on outside. Shaking the demon-possessed person's head back and forth has the same effect.

It can get crazy when you're called upon to cast a demon out of someone, so I learned to remember a simple acrostic: F-S-Y-S (Forehead, Stance, Yell, Shake).

FSYS works like a charm. Unless you actually believe demons exist (which I do) and you really want to help people. In that case FSYS is useless. But I was young, impressionable, and so overzealous I would have fallen for anything.

In the first half of 1986, my friends and I spent a lot of time going up to High Street on the campus of Ohio State and engaging in "street evangelism." All the campus bars are located on High Street, so we felt this was the perfect area to walk up to people and try to lead them to Christ on the spot. If we encountered someone who had a demon, we fell back on our FSYS training.

You would think that no sane person would respond positively to four college students confronting him or her about the claims of Christ on High Street, but we actually led a number of people to faith this way. In fact, the more people responded, the more we felt called to continue. We began spending just about every Friday and Saturday night walking High Street, leading people to Jesus.

Then it happened. It was bound to happen sooner or later.

In an alley off High Street, I stumbled upon a man lying on the ground. *Was he asleep? Was he dead? Was there foul play involved?* Lots of thoughts crossed my mind. After assessing the situation, I realized that this man was possessed by a demon. You might have concluded that his blood alcohol level had passed .20, causing him to lose control of his gross motor skills and black out. But Rod had taught me better—this man was possessed by the demon of alcohol. Fortunately I knew *exactly* what I needed to do.

I quickly collected my thoughts, took a deep breath, and recalled FSYS: Forehead, Stance, Yell, Shake. I placed my hand on the man's forehead, hunched over into as much of a Heisman stance as I could on the ground, and began shouting at the demon.

"Depart, thou foul demon!" I proclaimed. No response.

"Returneth to thy hellish abode!" I yelled louder.

Still no response.

"Ye hellish demon of iniquity, I *command* thee to leave this man's body!"

The man starting moving.

I'm finally getting somewhere, I thought.

"Leave him!" I screamed. "Leave his body, never to return!" I shouted at the top of my lungs. He started moaning.

I'm close, I thought, so I started shaking his head back and forth and repeatedly screamed, "I cast thee out in the name of Jesus! I cast thee out in the name of Jesus! I cast thee out in the name of Jesus!"

Suddenly the man sat up, took a swing at me, and yelled in a drunken stupor, "I'lll cast *youu* out in the naaame of Jsssuuzzzz!"

And I just about wet my pants.

"Leave me alone, I'm trying to get some sleep!" he yelled as I ran down the alley like a frightened child.

RELATIONSHIPS ARE THE KEY

I share all of this to make one point: We led lots of people to Jesus on High Street in 1986, but none of the decisions people made for Christ stuck.

We tried following up with people only to discover that not one person was following Christ within weeks of his or her decision. Not one person stuck. *Not one.*

In fact, if anything, our efforts probably had the opposite effect—rather than leading people to Jesus, we undoubtedly pushed scores of them further away from Him. For every person we helped make a decision, there were hundreds who were undoubtedly turned off by the freaky Christians who walked up and asked, "If you were to die tonight, do you know if you would go to heaven or hell?"

The most ridiculous phase I went through in 1986 wasn't the "I want to look like Bono" mullet I sported or my tour of duty as a caster-outer of demons, but the time I spent trying to lead people to Christ without first building an authentic relationship with them.

From my experience doing street evangelism outside the bars on High Street, I learned the third step to living with apocalyptic urgency and effectively sharing your faith: *To have any measure of success, you've got to build relationships first.*

Granted, you're highly unlikely to walk the streets as I did, evangelistically pouncing on poor unsuspecting souls, but you might be tempted to share your faith with someone you don't know very well at work or in your neighborhood.

Please don't.

Human beings are relational creatures. We buy things from people we trust and we trust people we know. We take advice from people we spend time with. During difficult times we lean on people whose names we actually remember. Life has taught us that strangers who try to get too close too quickly almost always have an agenda, so we politely (or not so politely) hold people we don't know at arm's length. Friends, though fewer in number, have access to our hearts, while people we don't know simply don't. It's human nature.

Educational leader Dr. James Comer contends, "No significant learning occurs without a significant relationship."[2] I wholeheartedly agree, especially when it comes to learning about Christ. Unless you have a relationship with the person you're trying to guide spiritually, they'll be as excited to hear you talk about God as they are when a telemarketer interrupts them during dinner. That's why, if you truly believe in hell, you must focus on building genuine relationships with people *before* you say anything to them about Jesus.

There are three essentials to building the kind of relationship that eventually earns us the right to talk to people about spiritual matters.

1. Get Off Thy Rump

The first essential may appear dreadfully obvious, but to build an authentic relationship with a non-Christian, you have to take the first step. I'm always shocked by how many Christians sit back and expect their non-Christian friends to come to them.

"Go and make disciples of all nations," Jesus said in Matthew 28:19. When He shared those final words with His disciples, they knew exactly what He meant: If people were going to find out the amazing news of what He accomplished on the cross, they were going to have to tell people about it. The world wasn't going to come to their doorstep; they had to go to the world.

That same command applies to us today, along with its implications. Christianity at its heart is a sending religion. God the Father sent Jesus to live among us (John 1:1, 14), and now Jesus sends us into the world to build relationships with people far from Him. So many people talk about whether or not they feel "called" to go talk to someone who isn't a Christian. That's never something that's discussed in Scripture. In fact, the command to "go" in Matthew 28:19 isn't even a command. In the original Greek it's a participle. "While you are going, make disciples" is a better translation. The act of going is assumed.

The Creator of heaven and earth is sending you to your neighbor's fence to say "hello." The risen Jesus, the One who bled, suffered, and died, calls you to walk over to that lunch table and ask if you can join your coworkers. The Holy Spirit, the presence of God in your heart, nudges you to introduce yourself to those parents on your child's sports team. It's not even a question of whether or not you should; that's already decided. The gospel is a missionary movement. Instead of hacking through a dense jungle with a machete to get to some remote tribe in Indonesia, God calls you to hack through your personal comfort zone and initiate a conversation with that person you always see at the gym.

Can I share something with you? I hate this about Christianity. I'm an introvert, plus I'm a real chicken. "Chicken" and "introvert" aren't the most ideal characteristics to have when God tells you to build relationships with people you don't know. I mention this because you might be in the same boat as I am. My wife, on the other hand, a natural extrovert, reads Jesus' words and thinks to herself, *No problem. I'm always looking to make new friends anyway.* I've never once thought about any activity that way, much less evangelism.

I've worked through this problem by realizing that being a disciple of Jesus is a call to suffer. And while I may not suffer to the point where I lose my life, I will suffer this inconvenience.

2. Pick Three

The second essential to building genuine friendships with nonbelievers is picking three people to focus on. That's it. Don't try to save the entire world. Just focus on three people. When you lead those three people to Christ, then you can shift your focus to three more non-Christians, and then three more after that. In the meantime, don't worry about going to the ends of the earth to reach people for Jesus. Your mission field exists within the network of relationships that you already have.

The "pick three" concept comes from the evangelistic strategy Jesus Himself used during His time on earth. Based on what we can see in the Gospels, it's obvious Jesus spent uneven amounts of time with three groups of people.

First, Jesus spent part of his time with what the Gospels refer to as "the crowds." Luke 6:17–18 tells us, "A large crowd of his disciples was there and a great number of people from all over." You have a "crowd" of people in your life too—people with names you have a hard time remembering, but whose faces you recognize. These are simply the random acquaintances you've bumped into over the years who've been drawn into your relational orbit.

Second, out of the crowd of disciples following Jesus, "He appointed twelve that they might be with him" (Mark 3:14). While Jesus never ignored the crowds, He increasingly spent His time focusing on these twelve men.

Finally, there was a third group—and that's Peter, James, and John—those commonly referred to as Jesus' "inner circle." At certain moments in Jesus' ministry, He allowed these three men access that no one else enjoyed. "After six days Jesus took with him Peter, James and John the brother of James, and led them up a high mountain by themselves" (Matt. 17:1). Presumably these three heard and saw things no one else was privileged to experience.

We notice a very clear pattern in the way Jesus spent time with the people He was guiding and teaching—He interacted with the crowd, focused on His disciples, and concentrated on His inner circle. To me this has always been a good rule of thumb. There are inevitably dozens of non-Christians I could try to build relationships with, but I've chosen to limit my efforts to getting to know just twelve of them, and ultimately picking three to pour myself into.

The key is focus. Unless you're single, an extreme extrovert, or the heir to a fortune of cash that lets you quit work, you won't be able to stay in touch with more than twelve non-Christians at a time, or spend quality time with more than three of them. It's just not going to happen. The reality is Jesus had all the time in the world at His disposal but still chose to order His life this way. That's not a bad example to follow.

3. Live Like a Pagan

The third essential to building genuine relationships with non-believers is making a concerted effort to live like the people you're trying to reach.

As I shared in the previous chapter, when we first moved to the suburbs of Philadelphia, I began coaching soccer as a way to meet people. I'll never forget my first coaches' meeting on a Wednesday night at the local township building. I showed up early and sat in the front row. As the room began to fill up, I introduced myself to the coaches sitting around me.

Ten minutes after our meeting started, a man walked to the front of the room and sat down at the head table. He was obviously one of the coaching coordinators; everyone greeted him as he came in.

As he sat down, something caught my eye.

Is that toner smudged on his forehead?

It is *toner on his forehead!*

Oh my gosh. That's hysterical. He's going to be so embarrassed.

Should I pass him a note? Should I walk up and whisper in his ear?

I knew that if I was in his situation, I would want someone to say something to me, but no one else in the room budged. Finally, just as I was getting ready to let this man know about his embarrassing predicament, another man sat down beside him with toner on his forehead as well!

I'm coaching with a bunch of imbeciles, I thought.

I turned around to see if any of the other coaches had noticed, and saw that most of them had toner on their foreheads as well.

Then it hit me: *Oh yeah, it's Ash Wednesday.*

Growing up in central Ohio, I wasn't exposed to Catholicism. There just weren't many Catholics in our area. When we moved to Philadelphia, I had to spend a great deal of time learning the lifestyle, attitudes, and beliefs of those who grew up in the Catholic Church. If I was going to reach nonbelievers, the majority of whom in our area are former Catholics, I needed to understand their spiritual backgrounds.

You need to study the people you want to reach. Why? Because in order to be effective, you need to live like the people you feel called to evangelize. The issue has to do with barriers. Think about it. So many barriers already exist between you and the nonbelievers you'd like to reach—how you view the world and everything in it—the last thing you want to do is create more cultural barriers they must cross in order to have a relationship with you.

Call to mind the names of three potential non-Christians you could genuinely befriend. What do they wear? Where do they eat? What TV shows do they watch? How do they talk? What kind of technology do they use?

Now, compare how *you* live with how *they* live: Do you wear what they wear? Eat what they eat? Watch the TV shows they watch? Talk like they talk? Use the technology they use?

If you want to reach these people, you need to try to live like them. Missionaries call this "contextualization," which simply means presenting the gospel in the language and culture of those we're trying to reach. When missionaries go to a foreign country, they adopt everything about that country's culture—language, dress, etc. They do that to remove any potential barriers to sharing the gospel. They know the gospel itself can be enough of a barrier; they don't need to erect any more. You have the same task.

Speaking of this very issue, the apostle Paul wrote,

> Though I am free and belong to no one, I have made myself a slave to everyone, to win as many as possible. To the Jews I became like a Jew, to win the Jews. To those under the law I became like one under the law (though I myself am not under the law), so as to win those under the law. To those not having the law I became like one not having the law (though I am not free from God's law but am under Christ's law), so as to win those not having the law. To the weak I became weak, to win the weak. I have become all things to all people so that by all possible means I might save some. (1 Cor. 9:19–22)

Whether Paul was preaching the message of Jesus in Israel (a predominantly Jewish culture), or in Athens (an entirely pagan culture), he adapted himself to the people he was trying to reach. Notice the way Paul calls himself a slave ("I have made myself a slave to everyone"). That was Paul's way of stating that the burden of change falls upon the shoulders of the Christians, not those they are trying to reach.

We are the ones who should feel uncomfortable and inconvenienced, not the non-Christians we're trying to reach. The best way I know how to put it is this: You should do everything short of sin to live exactly like the people with whom you're trying to build a relationship.

What that means to me is that I go to parties where there's lots of drinking. That's what non-Christians in our area, many from Catholic backgrounds, often do—they get together and drink and socialize. I myself don't drink, but I make a point to spend time with those who do. Some Christians would frown on that. That's okay; I'm not trying to evangelize Christians.

I also hang out with guys who drop F-bombs left and right, and they feel totally comfortable around me when they do it because I don't judge them in any way. I am obviously not using the same language, but I don't judge them. Peter, James, and John surely had their own swear words, but I don't remember Jesus coming uncorked on them for their salty language.

The reason I don't say anything to them is I don't want to win the battle (getting them to stop swearing) but lose the war (miss the opportunity to share Christ because they think I'm judgmental).

My goal isn't simply to "become all things to all people" because it's some manipulative trick to get them to drop their guard. I truly want friendships with them. As the apostle Paul told the believers he led to Christ in the ancient city of Thessalonica, "We were delighted to share with you not only the gospel of God but our lives as well" (1 Thess. 2:8). That's my goal—I genuinely want to share my life with those I'm trying to befriend. Is it my goal to eventually lead them to faith in Christ? Of course. But that doesn't mean my intent to become their friend isn't genuine.

But we'll never get the chance to develop friendships with non-believers if they think we're odd.

That's why I read the same newspapers they read.

I try to eat at the same restaurants they do.

I try to dress the way they dress.

I listen to the same music and watch the same TV shows.

The list goes on and on.

Paul wrote, "I have become all things to all people so that by all possible means I might save some" (1 Cor. 9:22).

What that means to me is one thing—*just be normal.*

WHAT NONBELIEVERS REALLY NEED

So far we've talked about three action steps that we need to take to lead those within our circles of influence to Christ. The first step is to find something you're interested in that makes *you* interesting. The second step is to chill out and not come on too strong with those you want to reach. In this chapter we talked about a third step: focusing on building authentic relationships.

You'll notice that not once have I told you what to say. That's by design. My strategy, if it's fair to talk about it as a "strategy" at all, is simply to focus on relationships. Relationships *are* the strategy.

My rule of thumb is, barring unusual circumstances, I don't even share that I'm a Christian until I'm asked. I believe my job is to strip all the oddities of the Christian subculture away from my life and love those I'm befriending so intensely and graciously that they bring it up first. I figure that in most circumstances if I'm living the way I should be living, I'm going to stand out like an NBA basketball player walking down the hallway of an elementary school. By the time someone asks about my faith, the person is usually ready for me to share the gospel.

George Whitefield was one of the key figures in bringing about what historians call The Great Awakening, an eighteenth-century religious revival that swept across the United States and Britain. In his sermon called "Jacob's Ladder," Whitefield said, "God forbid that I should travel with anybody a quarter of an hour without speaking of Christ to them."[3]

No disrespect to Whitefield, but that's one of the dumbest things I've ever heard.

Before you ever open your mouth to talk about Jesus, ask yourself, "Do I have a relationship with this person?" If you don't, you're not ready.

In 1986, after spending an evening evangelizing on High Street, my friends and I went to eat pizza. It was one o'clock in the morning, and after we ordered, we noticed a former high-school classmate of ours sitting alone on the other side of the restaurant. We were still jazzed about sharing our faith just a few hours before, so we went over to talk to him about God as well.

He had not heard that I'd become a Christian since graduating high school, so it was kind of cool sharing the story of the way God was changing my life. Then out of nowhere I asked him, "Why don't you become a Christian, Rich? Is there anything that's stopping you?"

"I don't know," I remember him saying. "I have so many questions. I don't even know if I believe in God."

Fortunately we were full of answers.

For almost two straight hours my friend and I tag teamed our spiritually questioning acquaintance. No question was too difficult. Each of his hesitations we perceived as a sign that we needed to share more information—not that he needed more time to process what we'd already shared.

"Today is the day of salvation," we kept telling him. "This is your moment to get your life back on track."

Finally, around 3:00 a.m., he caved in and said, "Okay, I'm in."

Then I did what any normal Christian would do on a Friday night at 3:00 a.m.—I broke into the church I grew up in and baptized my friend.

Because we didn't want to wait (for fear that Rich might change his mind), we took a crowbar from my trunk, pried a window open, and shimmied inside. Once inside we walked into the baptistery and I baptized Rich.

It was surreal.

We hugged.

We shouted.

We celebrated.

Then, because it was late, I gave our new brother in Christ the Bible I was using at the time and took him home. It was one of the coolest evangelistic moments of my life.

Ten years later I bumped into Rich's brother while traveling through my hometown to see family. Just a few weeks after leading Rich to Christ and baptizing him at 3:00 a.m., I headed off to school and lost touch with him, so I was excited to catch up on the past decade.

"How is Rich doing?" I asked.

"Not so well, I'm afraid. In 1986 he went to jail for possession of cocaine, and when he got out he fathered a couple kids and has been bouncing around from job to job ever since. In the meantime I have come to the Lord and have been praying for him ever since. He's just a really lost person right now."

I was heartbroken.

"You know, I led your brother to Christ that summer. I baptized him at three a.m. in our church's baptistery. It was a pretty amazing experience."

"I know that," he said. "Rich told me. He was really touched that you did that for him."

"If you don't mind me asking, what happened?"

He looked away for a moment, and then said something I've never forgotten.

"I guess what Rich needed more than baptism at that time was a friend."

NOTES

1. Joe Aldrich, quoted in Bill Hybels and Mark Mittelberg, *Becoming a Contagious Christian* (Grand Rapids, MI: Zondervan, 1994), 54.

2. James Comer (lecture given at Education Service Center, Region IV, Houston, TX, quoted in Pete Hall, Alisa Simeral, *Building Teachers' Capacity for Success* (Alexandria, VA: Association for Supervision and Curriculum Development, 2008), 16.

3. George Whitefield, "Jacob's Ladder," in *Selected Sermons of George Whitefield* (London: Religious Tract Society, 1904), 158.

12

DOORS

The weight of this sad time we must obey; Speak
what we feel, not what we ought to say.

—*Shakespeare,* King Lear[1]

The real art of sharing your faith is knowing when to open your mouth and when to shut it.

My struggle has always been a tendency to speak about Christ when I should keep silent, or to keep silent when I should speak up. It's hard sometimes to figure out the appropriate moment to initiate a spiritual conversation. What makes matters worse is that it's hard to know when to say certain things period, whether it's talking about God or sending an undercooked steak back to the chef. Knowing what to say, and when to say it, is an art.

I'll never forget my first preaching class at Cincinnati Christian University.[2] Lisa and I had just gotten married and moved to Cincinnati so that she could finish the final year of her undergrad degree at the University of Cincinnati and I could finish my degree at CCU. I was new to the school and felt a little nervous about not knowing anyone. Fortunately, when I walked into my first class, Advanced Preaching, I made a few friends and began to feel more comfortable.

Our first assignment was rather intimidating: Deliver a twenty-five-minute sermon on a Bible passage of our choosing, and then receive evaluation from the rest of the class.

The day came when we had to preach our first sermons. Since I was new to the school and had never heard my fellow classmates speak, I didn't know what to expect. The professor passed out our evaluation forms as we sat expectantly, waiting to begin.

Five minutes into the first student's sermon, I looked around and thought to myself, *Is this a joke? What the heck is going on here?* It was like when a horrible singer auditions for *American Idol* and the judges start laughing and hiding their faces.

It was *that* bad.

I mean it was *really* bad.

I kid you not—I literally thought it was a practical joke.

But I realized quickly that it wasn't a joke.

I had transferred into this school halfway through my degree program, so I'd already taken five or six preaching classes. I thought that by the time you reach Advanced Preaching either you can preach, or you can't. Am I right?

As I looked around, I couldn't understand why everyone else couldn't see what I was seeing. They hung on this guy's every word—smiling, nodding their heads, and laughing really hard at his horrible jokes.

It was obvious that he had spent two years of his life trying to become a preacher, and no one ever cared enough to tell him the truth.

He fell over his words. Incoherent statements shot out of his mouth. Awkward pauses littered his entire talk.

Have you ever heard a sermon and thought to yourself, *Surely someone early on had to hear this guy preach. Why didn't they just come out and encourage him to pursue another area of ministry? Or another occupation altogether?*

I realized I had a decision to make—say something or keep silent. I chose to say something. This was about to become that moment of encouragement.

As he walked off the podium, I began filling out my evaluation form, starting with the positive comments first:

Positive:

- This is the first time I've ever heard you preach—it's nice to meet you.
- I love the fact that you want to preach.
- You had a nice suit on. (By this point I scratched my head, trying to find more positive things to say.)
- Good job reading the passage before the sermon started.
- You ended on time. That's really tough to do! Good job.

Then I went on to my "constructive" comments:

Constructive:

- I have to be honest—that was really rough to listen to.

- You didn't maintain eye contact with anyone. You looked down the whole time.
- I don't want to hurt your feelings, but I still have no idea what you were talking about—did you have a point you wanted to get across? Maybe it would help to simply say, "Here's what I'm trying to say," and then say it.
- Long, awkward pauses.
- Not sure what the grunting was about. The weird noises—I'm not sure if you were clearing your throat or what—but that was really distracting. That should be easy to fix though.
- Jokes weren't really funny. (Then I wrestled with whether or not I should say any more. In the end, I decided I needed to be honest.)
- I say this as lovingly as I can—you might want to consider whether or not preaching is something you really want to do for the rest of your life. You were in a LOT of pain up there. It was hard to watch. Is there something you could do in ministry you would enjoy more?

Our professor asked the student who preached the sermon to leave the room, and then walked to the front of the room.

"Please pass your evaluation forms to the front of the class," he said. After collecting the forms, he stood silently for a moment, staring at the back wall. Seconds later his eyes welled up with tears.

"I want you to know that I consider that message nothing short of a miracle!"

Huh?

"When he first came to this school, he couldn't stand up to speak without throwing up beforehand. But he came to me one day and said, 'I want to preach the gospel, will you help me?' I said, 'Son, God can use anybody with a heart like yours.'"

Oh no, I thought, and started to slide down into my seat.

"I took him under my wing and had him take every class I offered."

"Please, God, no," I murmured under my breath as I recalled all the comments I had just written down.

"His first sermon, he almost fainted."

Oh man.

"When he gave his second sermon, he ran out afterward and threw up in the restroom."

I'm feeling sick to my stomach myself, I thought. *I need to get my form back.*

"But he kept working. Before class—after class—late at night—it didn't matter; he put his heart and soul into preaching and has become my most committed student."

Dear God, kill me now, I closed my eyes and prayed.

To cap off my misery, the professor slowly wiped a tear from his eye and said, "Class, the sermon he just delivered was without question one of the highlights of my entire career teaching young preachers to preach. I am *so* proud of that young man. Now, let's read those evaluations together as a class!"

I closed my eyes and slowly put my face down on my desktop.

LOOK FOR THE OPEN DOOR

Which do you struggle with more: opening your mouth when it should stay closed, or keeping your mouth closed when it should open up?

More than likely, like me, you struggle with both. There are probably times when you've wished you *hadn't* said something when you did. Then there are probably times when you wished you *had* spoken up, but didn't. And perhaps you've been in a situation like my Advanced Preaching class, when you said something you regretted at the time, and even though you felt bad afterward you weren't quite sure what you would have said differently.

Sharing our faith poses similar challenges: How early in the relationship with nonbelievers should we bring up God? And when we do, what should we say? What happens after that initial discussion? What do we share after that? How often can we talk about Jesus without risking becoming a caricature of the weird, pushy Christian? Finally, how do we "close the deal," as some might say?

The simple answer to all of these questions is: You have to find out for yourself. Evangelism really is an art. There are as many ways to share your faith as there are Christians on the planet. The good thing though is that there is a spiritual principle that will help you find your way.

After years struggling to figure out when to open my mouth and when to keep silent, I've learned a fourth step to effectively sharing my faith: *Look for the open door.*

I draw this principle from Paul's powerful words in Colossians 4:2–6:

> Devote yourselves to prayer, being watchful and thankful. And pray for us, too, that God may open a door for our message, so that we may proclaim the mystery of Christ, for which I am in chains. Pray that I may proclaim it clearly, as I should. Be wise in the way you act toward outsiders; make the most of every opportunity. Let your conversation be always full of grace, seasoned with salt, so that you may know how to answer everyone.

The key to knowing when to speak and when to keep silent is found in the metaphor of the open door. This biblical metaphor refers to the divinely generated opportunities that God places before each of us throughout our lives.

Over the years I've noticed that at certain times, for no apparent reason, someone will open themselves up to a spiritual conversation. They'll ask a question, or I'll notice a slight pause in the middle of a conversation, and that's when I realize I have an open-door opportunity.

Whenever I sense an open door and walk through it to talk about Christ, amazing things happen. Barriers fall away. Hearts become soft. Hurts are healed. Questions are answered. Without a doubt, the most important thing you and I can do to discern when to speak about Christ is to look for an open door.

WHY DOORS OPEN

It's rare to find someone who isn't a Christian who wants to talk about God. The average nonbeliever has often built up so much resistance that it seems to take a supernatural work of God to find someone willing to have a spiritual conversation. That's why Paul said we should pray for doors to open. Evangelistic doors are only opened by the supernatural. "Devote yourselves to prayer, being watchful and thankful. And pray for us, too, that God may open a door for our message" (Col. 4:2–3).

Pray.

Devote yourself to prayer.

Be watchful as you pray.

That's when you'll notice doors starting to open all around you.

The great Chinese spiritual writer Watchman Nee wrote, "Our prayers thus lay the track down on which God's power can come. Like some mighty locomotive, His power is irresistible, but it cannot reach us without rails."[3]

I try to make it a habit to pray every single day for the three people I've been led by God to befriend and try to lead to Christ. I say that I "try" to make it a habit to pray because, quite honestly, many days I forget. Here's what I've noticed though—when I don't forget, the wildest things start to happen.

When I pray, people ask me random questions at seemingly odd times. Events converge forcing one of these friends and me to spend more time together. Appointments change. Hearts soften. God moves.

In short, doors open.

For instance, a number of years ago I began praying for an atheist friend of mine who is a scientist. I connected with him through our common interest in hiking. He didn't believe in anything at the time, let alone God.

Lisa and I had plans to go out to dinner and a movie with him and his wife (who was a Christian). The week prior, I prayed every day that God would open up a door to share something with him that would remove one of the barriers standing in the way of his receiving Christ.

At dinner our wives talked about school, which led to kids, which led to after-school activities, which eventually led to a discussion about church. Then he spoke up.

"I just don't understand why this religion business is so important to you three," he said.

His wife jumped in immediately and began talking about how religion was important to teach positive values to the kids.

"I agree. That's why I go to church with you," he said. "I just don't believe in any of it."

Then it happened—I sensed that a door had opened. Nothing mystical happened. No angel dust fell around the room. I didn't get a funny, warm feeling all over my body. I just sensed I was supposed to say something, so I did.

"Honestly, I think most churches do a pretty mediocre job at teaching kids values," I said. "In fact, I think you can be a person with positive values and never set foot in a church. The way I understand it, Christianity is about helping people get to heaven. Learning positive values is secondary to that."

Once I said that we were off to the races.

He became animated and fired questions at me like a police officer interrogating a suspect. After every statement I made he came back with two rebuttals he had waiting in the wings. His wife commented later she had never seen him get so engaged in a discussion about religion in their entire marriage.

My friend's problem was that he felt that he was good enough to get to heaven, if there was such a place, based simply on his being a good person.

"Listen, I know I'm not going to be able to make you believe what the Bible teaches is true by the time we finish our cheesecake, but let me at least make sure you understand what it is that I'm saying." I took his glass of ice water and moved it to one side of the table, and then I took my glass and moved it to the other side.

"Imagine this glass over here to my left—that's you. Now imagine this glass to my right—that's God. The Bible says because of the things you've done in your life (the Bible calls it sin) you have offended God's holy nature and created a pretty big rift between the two of you. The space in between these glasses represents that rift. Got the image?"

"Got it," he said.

"How are you going to get back over to God's side?"

"By being a good person. He'll let me in."

"Really?" I took a pack of sugar and said, "This sugar packet represents Mother Teresa. Let's imagine she took what I call 'the goodness long jump.' Based on her being a good person alone, how far do you think she would be able to jump across this chasm to get over to God's side?"

"All the way?"

"Nice try. The Bible says she would fall *way* short. But since she's Mother Teresa, arguably one of the most godly people of the twentieth century, let's imagine her 'goodness long jump' takes her halfway across."

Then I took the packet of sugar and placed it in between the two glasses.

"Here's my next question," I said as I grabbed a packet of Splenda. "This Splenda is you. Based on your goodness alone, how far do you think you would make it across the chasm between you and God?"

He grabbed the packet and put it next to Mother Teresa.

His wife burst out laughing. "This is Mother Teresa we're talking about!"

Then she grabbed the packet and moved it way back.

"Here's the central idea behind Christianity," I continued. "Your sin has made it impossible for you to make it over to God's side. You need help. What's worse is the Bible says that if you don't fix this problem by the time you die, you will stay separated from God, forever. The Bible calls that hell."

Then I let that sink in for a moment and asked him one more question, "Do you believe this?"

Long pause.

"I believe in Star Trek."

"What does that mean?"

"Something's out there. I just don't know what it is yet."

"Fair enough," I said. "But hopefully the USS *Enterprise* can get us to the movie in time, because all this talk about God you started is going to make us late."

He laughed, we paid the check, and then drove as fast as we could to get over to the theater.

As it turned out, the only movie that wasn't sold out was one starring Jodie Foster and Matthew McConaughey called *Contact.* Even though it's been years since the movie came out, and I'm sure you probably saw it, I won't spoil the plot and details just in case you haven't seen it. All I will say is that Jodie Foster plays a scientist who happens to be an atheist, just like my friend. And by the end of the movie she experiences something that shakes her to the core. Simply put—it was one of the most compelling movies about faith and science I've ever seen.

We walked out of the theater and the first words out of my friend's mouth were, "You set me up."

I smiled.

I didn't set my friend up. God did.

The only thing I did was devote myself to prayer, and God did the rest.

WHAT TO DO WHEN DOORS OPEN

I take it as a divine leading from God that until I sense an evangelistic door opening, I keep my mouth shut. That's what I meant in the previous chapter when I mentioned that I say nothing to nonbelievers about whether I'm a Christian or not until they ask me first. I don't want to try to speak when my mouth should be shut, or to carry the metaphor a little further along—walk into a closed door. Theologian Lewis Chafer wrote, "When led of the Spirit, the child of God must be as ready to wait as to go, as prepared to be silent as to speak."[4]

I live by that.

Practically speaking, that has meant that for some friendships I've waited close to a year before the subject of Christianity ever came up. Parents on my soccer team regularly walked up to me after their daughter had been on my team for an entire year and said, "I had no idea you were the pastor of Christ's Church of the Valley. All my friends go there."

Why didn't I say anything?

The answer is very simple—no door had opened yet.

Until a door opens, I say nothing. I mean that. I give no indication at all through what I say (but hopefully I do through my behavior) that I'm a Christian. I focus on doing that thing I'm interested in (in this case coaching soccer), doing it with people I'm trying to reach, chilling out, and building genuine relationships.

However, you had better believe that I'm always prayerfully and patiently looking for the slightest crack to open in the doorway to that person's heart. When that happens, I'm through it faster than an Olympic sprinter.

Colossians 4:4–6 tells us that there are two specific things all Christians should do when God opens up a door with their non-believing friends.

1. Speak Clearly

Let me share a story about what it's like for most non-Christians when a Christian attempts to share Christ unannounced and with no prior relationship.

When I was thirteen years old my parents must have noticed that my body was changing and the fact that I'd become more interested in girls, because one day my mom walked into my bedroom unannounced and handed me an antiquated booklet called "A Valuable Sex Guide for Father and Son."

I took one look at the booklet, then looked back at my mom and said, "Are you kidding me? What is this, like, one hundred years old or something?"

My mom said, "If you have any questions, talk to your dad."

And that was my sex talk.

The first thing I noticed was a line that said it was "A Completely New 1944–45 Edition." Oh boy.

Then I flipped it over and looked at the index—and was horrified—first that my mom gave it to me, and second that my eyes had to read things like what was on page ten:

> SELF-ABUSE, injures health and character, causes impotency 10

I had no idea what "self-abuse" meant. Curious, I turned to the page and cringed. It was referring to the *"M* word." I'm still in therapy over this whole experience.

I bring this up because this can be what it's like for most nonbelievers when their Christian friends jump at the chance to talk to them about Christ. The nonbeliever asks a simple question, and the Christian blindsides him or her with an old book and a very serious conversation about the heavy implications for not paying attention. Oftentimes the nonbeliever becomes confused, slightly embarrassed, and leaves the conversation no closer to figuring out the path back to God than when he or she asked the original question.

Colossians 4:4 says, "Pray that I may proclaim it clearly, as I should."

Your first job when you walk through that open door is to speak *clearly* about "the mystery of Christ" (v. 3), so that when you're done talking it's no longer a mystery.

Can you do that? I've found it helpful to come up with a visual image that will stick in people's minds, like the goodness long jump, or the one a friend of mine once used with me.

When I was in ninth grade my friend Deron Brickey became a Christian. I'll never forget sitting at the lunch table two days later and hearing him ask me, "Brian, are you are Christian?"

"Of course I'm a Christian," I replied. "I go to church."

Deron shot back, "I didn't ask you if you go to church. I asked you if you are a Christian. Going to church doesn't make you a Christian any more than sitting in a garage makes you a car."

The moment Deron spoke those words, that metaphor seared into my consciousness.

Four years later, when Deron eventually helped me cross the line of faith, it was that image that had made it crystal clear to me the difference between attending religious services and giving one's life to Christ. That's your job. Make it clear. Speak so clearly that when you're done speaking, the mystery of Christ is no longer a mystery.

Please understand that this is a huge responsibility. As Matthew 13:19 points out, "When anyone hears the message about the kingdom and does not understand it, the evil one comes and snatches away what was sown in their heart."

If people don't understand what you're trying to say once you're finished speaking, there's no guarantee that door may ever open up again for you. That's why whenever a door opens, I usually ask, "Has anyone ever told you about the central idea of Christianity?"

Then I'll share the goodness long jump, or some other image that will help sear that central truth in their mind forever.

As Paul put it, "Make the most of every opportunity" (Col. 4:5).

2. Speak to Their Deepest Hunger

Colossians 4:6 says, "Let your conversation be always full of grace, seasoned with salt." Salt is an interesting image in this context. In the ancient Near East, salt was primarily a preservative, as it is in many parts of the world today, but it was also used for flavoring. I believe that's the meaning intended in this passage. Paul is telling us that when God opens up an evangelistic door, it's our job to connect the message of Christ to our lost friend's deepest hunger.

I've learned that pain is the hinge upon which doors swing open. Everyone experiences pain. You have pain in your life and I have pain in my life. The difference between what we experience as Christians and what our nonbelieving friends experience is this: They experience pain *without* the presence of God. We have the gift of God's Holy Spirit living inside of us. We are empowered. We are filled with hope. We can walk with strength even in our darkest hours.

Non-Christians don't experience this in the same way. That's why, when I'm building friendships with nonbelievers, I often try to peel back the layers of their lives to uncover the pain. Find the pain and you'll find their area of greatest hunger.

Our most trusted tools in this regard are personal transparency, asking questions, and listening. I've always found that the more transparent I am with the junk in my life, the more transparent non-Christians are with me.

I'll never forget the time I was driving in the car with a nonbelieving friend of mine when he asked me to pray for him.

"Sorry, can't do it."

"Why?" he asked.

"Because God and I aren't on speaking terms right now. I'm so ticked off about my dad having cancer that I haven't prayed in two weeks."

He just sat there. I guess he didn't expect me to be so forthcoming. Then, after a long, awkward silence, he said, "I'm with you, man." I looked over at him and smiled.

We rode in the car for about another hour, listening to the radio and making small talk. Then out of nowhere he opened up about all the stuff going on in his life—problems with his wife, troubles at work, and anxiety about his son—and I just listened. I sat there and simply listened, occasionally asking a question or two.

When we got to where we were headed, he sort of capped off everything he was saying by telling me, "It's hard sometimes to believe in God, as you well know."

"You're not kidding," I said.

As we opened the car doors to get out I said, "Let me share one of my all-time favorite quotes. It's gotten me through a lot of stuff over the years. Tuck it away and remember it the next time you're feeling down. It's from a Spanish philosopher named Miguel de Unamuno. He wrote,

> Those who believe they believe in God, but without passion in the heart, without anguish of mind, without uncertainty, without doubt, and even at times without despair, believe only in the idea of God, and not in God himself.[5]

"What you're going through right now isn't evidence that God doesn't exist," I said. "Your pain is evidence that we are loved by a God who knows what it's like to suffer firsthand."

"Yeah, I know," he said. "I'm starting to believe that."

And that was that.

I smiled. He patted me on the back. And as he closed his car door, I knew that a spiritual door was starting to open.

NOTES

1. William Shakespeare, *King Lear,* in *The Complete Works of William Shakespeare: The Cambridge Text,* ed. William Aldis Wright (London: Cambridge University Press, 1980), 5.3.324–5. References are to act, scene, and line.

2. Cincinnati Christian University was formerly known as Cincinnati Bible College and Seminary.

3. Watchman Nee, quoted in Terrance Tiessen, *Providence & Prayer* (Downers Grove, IL: InterVarsity Press, 2000), 127.

4. Lewis Sperry Chafer, "Christian Quotes on Obedience to God," *Daily Christian Quote,* http://dailychristianquote.com/dcqobedience2.html.

5. Miguel de Unamuno, quoted in Madeleine L'Engle, *Walking on Water* (New York: North Point, 1995), 32.

AFTERWORD: LOVE

Being an extrovert isn't essential to
evangelism—obedience and love are.
—Rebecca Manley Pippert[1]

The first car Lisa and I bought together was a 1975 Datsun B210.

Just to be precise, I actually brought a car *into* our marriage—a high-powered chick magnet called a 1988 Ford Escort. That car wasn't even considered a regular Ford Escort. It was the completely stripped down base model Ford Escort, called a *Pony*, complete with stick shift, manual windows, and manual door locks.

We had just gotten married and both of us worked and went to school full-time, but in addition to that, Lisa was getting ready to begin student teaching. If we didn't do something about our "one car situation," soon one of us would be stranded.

I looked in the newspaper but couldn't find anything we could afford.

As I shared my dilemma with a friend at work, a coworker of ours overhead us talking.

"I've got what you're looking for," my friend Marty said.

"What's that?"

"My wife's making me, er, I mean, asking me to sell my car. It's everything you're looking for—cheap with good gas mileage. I'll show it to you."

We walked outside to the parking lot.

"Here it is," he said, pointing to the green Datsun B210 covered with rust.

I burst out laughing!

"Are you kidding me, Marty? This car isn't green, it's rust colored! There's more rust on the car than paint!"

"Granted, the exterior is a little rough, but—"

"A *little* rough? It looks like you keep it parked in a pool full of battery acid!"

"Wait till you drive it. You'll like it."

He unlocked the door and got behind the steering wheel.

"Okay, now this may seem a little weird, but the ignition switch wasn't working, so I pulled it out of the steering column and duct taped it to the dashboard."

"Oh, this keeps getting better!"

"So what you have to do is use the end of a fork to start the car."

"The end of a fork?"

At this point I could barely contain myself. I laughed so hard tears were streaming down my cheeks.

"It's simple: Put your foot on the clutch, punch the gas, turn the fork, and the car will start."

It was the funniest example of do-it-yourself automotive maintenance I had ever seen.

"Hop in and let's take her for a spin."

I sat in the passenger's seat and we drove off.

"What's that smell?" I asked.

"Oh, that's the engine."

"Is something wrong?"

"Oh no, the engine is fine. That smell is from fumes coming through the floorboard."

I looked down and yelled, "*What the heck?*"

The floorboard had huge holes rusted through it. You could literally see the road as you were driving.

"Okay," Marty said as he began laughing with me. "Yes. Okay. Most people would look at the floorboards and say, 'This is a deal breaker.' But I see the holes as a positive. Have you ever tried to park and weren't sure where the yellow lines were? In other cars you have to look out the window to find them. In this car all you have to do is look down!"

"Let's cut to the chase," I said. "What's your price?"

"I've got about five hundred in it, but because we're friends, I'll sell it to you for two hundred."

I looked at the fork sticking out of the ignition and the massive holes in the floorboards and balanced that with how much money I had to spend. I reached over, shook his hand, and said, "Deal."

And that's how I became the proud owner of a thirteen-year-old, rusted-out 1975 Datsun B210.

Believe it or not, I loved that car. It was reliable and got great gas mileage. The only problem was Lisa wouldn't drive it because it made her teaching outfits smell like gasoline. I didn't complain. Even though it wasn't warm in the winter (because of the cold air whipping through the floorboards), it turned out to be a pretty good car.

Then, as luck would have it, the alternator went bad.

With very little money to fix it, a friend offered to help me pick out a new alternator. But when he put the alternator in, he forgot to disconnect the wiring from the battery, and the car's electrical system instantly shorted out, causing smoke to billow out of the engine. My $200 Datsun B210 equipped with a brand-new $43 alternator was now worthless.

We pushed the car to the curb in front of my friend's house, and I told him that I would have someone tow it to the junkyard. Unfortunately I was busy, so two days turned into two weeks, and eventually a month went by.

I'll get to it, I thought. *As long as my friend doesn't bug me, I have plenty of time.*

I was wrong.

One day we got an official-looking letter from the Cincinnati Police Department informing me that a warrant had been issued for my arrest. The car had been impounded, I had failed to show up for court, and the judge had issued a warrant.

Minutes later I was on the phone trying to figure out what in the world was going on. The person on the line told me I had two options. I could either pay a four hundred dollar fine, or do nothing and the sheriff would take me to jail. After pushing her a bit she shared that I had a third option: I could show up to a court date and fight the charges.

Two weeks later I was standing before the judge.

The courtroom was intimidating. The long, narrow room had an entrance on one side where the defendants came in and found a seat. On the other end stood an old wooden railing that stretched across the room, creating a barrier between the people and the judge. Behind the railing perched the judge, sitting a few feet off the ground behind a large desk. One by one the bailiff read the names of the defendants whose cases were next in line.

Those of us whose cases were second, third, and fourth in the docket had to stand up, get in line, and prepare to address the judge.

"Keep it moving," the bailiff yelled. Eventually it was my turn to get in line. I turned to Lisa with a raised eyebrow and said, "Here goes."

If the room itself was intimidating, that's only because it reflected the personality of the judge. He was tough. Every time someone in front of me made excuses, he yelled and handed down the stiffest penalty possible.

Twenty minutes later the bailiff called my name and case:

> *The City of Cincinnati v. Brian Jones*
> Abandonment of vehicle on city property. Failure
> to appear in court.
> Warrant issued.

The judge shuffled his papers in front of him as he cleared his throat.

"Do you understand the charges being brought against you?"

"Yes, I do, sir," I said with a slight tremor in my voice. (Lisa calls it my nervous voice—I get it when I stand before judges, or when I forget to put the toilet seat down.)

"What do you have to say for yourself?"

"Your Honor," I replied. "My wife and I are both in college. We don't have any money, but she's doing student teaching, so I bought a cheap car from a friend. It broke down. I left it in front of a friend's house. I thought that was legal to do that. I did get the court summons in the mail to appear, but by that time it was too—"

The judge cut me off.

"It's a city street. Who do you think maintains those streets—your friend?"

"Sir, it was an error in judgment. I ask for your mercy."

"I'll waive all the other actions against you, but the fine stands at four hundred dollars."

"Sir, I don't have four hundred dollars. The car cost me two hundred."

"Two hundred?"

"Yes. It was a piece of junk."

"A piece of junk that you left on my street."

"Yeah, I know, but that was a genuine mistake. Please, sir. Can you forgive the fine?"

Long pause.

"You're lucky I'm in a lenient mood today, son. I'll waive the four hundred."

"Yes!" I yelled as I pumped my fist in the air.

I couldn't believe it. One minute I'm thinking I'm going to jail to pay off a fine, the next minute the debt was forgiven.

"Hold on," he said. "Don't celebrate so fast. There is a forty-dollar fee to process the paperwork so your car can be taken to the junkyard. Can you afford that?"

I looked at Lisa and smiled. We had only thirty-five dollars in our bank account to get us until the next payday. I shrugged my shoulders and said, "I'm afraid not, Your Honor. Do you have a payment plan?"

He chuckled and said, "Three equal payments of $13.33 spread out over the next three months. Case closed."

THE FINAL STEP

We've come now to the final part of the book. We've definitely covered a lot of ground together. In the first part of the book we explored why Christians stop believing in hell, even in the face of strong biblical support. And then we searched the Scriptures to help us understand why hell exists in the first place, and how knowing this truth fills us with apocalyptic urgency to reach the lost. Finally, I spent the last four chapters outlining a few simple action steps for you to follow so you can begin reaching those within your circle of influence.

After all the time we've spent together, I have just one last thing I'd like to share with you: You can do this.

You really can.

You can help save your nonbelieving friends from hell.

I've been a pastor for a long time now, and over the years I've met thousands of Christians who believe in everything we've talked about—heaven, hell, God's wrath, Jesus' death as propitiation, our responsibility to share what we know with non-Christians—but they've never led anyone to Christ. Not a single person.

They all share similar reasons why:

"I'm scared."

"I don't know enough."

"I'm an introvert."

"I'm afraid I'll do something wrong."

What's interesting is that they all believe that, just like I had to stand before a judge in Cincinnati to plead my case, their nonbelieving family and friends will stand before God. They don't dispute that fact at all. They also believe that their friends aren't getting off the hook. Without Christ, they know that there will be no leniency, no spiritual payment plan after death to redeem all the wrong they did in this life. They believe in hell. They believe in evangelism. They feel apocalyptic urgency. They just don't evangelize.

Does this describe you?

If it does, I want you to know that you can do this.

You can.

Every single Christian can.

Here's the final action step to living with apocalyptic urgency and effectively sharing you faith: *Just love people.*

That's it.

Just love people.

Whenever you find yourself rubbing shoulders with people far from God, and you don't know what to say or do, when all else fails, just love them. Summing up why he was willing to suffer so much to reach people far from God, the apostle Paul wrote, "Christ's love compels us" (2 Cor. 5:14).

My fear is that you might walk away from our discussion about hell with the wrong image of God stuck in your mind—that God is dispassionately sitting behind a large wooden desk in an imposing courtroom, waiting for Jesus to call people to come forward and hear their sentence. Some get into heaven, some don't. The decision is cold, direct, and to the point. God is utterly detached and unmoved by the verdict He renders.

That's a distortion. There's no image like that in Scripture. When the collective witness of Scripture is taken into account, the most accurate image of God is that of the father of the prodigal son. This father doesn't sit behind a desk. He paces back and forth, night after night, worried sick about the fact that His child has left home. The last thing He feels is emotional distance. Rather, He is so distraught over the prospect of losing His child that He's unwilling to eat and unable to think straight.

That's the God we serve.

As Richard Foster so aptly described Him, "The heart of God is an open wound of love."[2]

God isn't a judge sitting up in the sky, gleefully waiting to send bad people to hell. "For God so *loved* the world," John 3:16 says, "that he gave his one and only Son, that whoever believes in him shall not perish but have eternal life."

God loves us. He genuinely, deeply, and irrationally loves us. Strike that image of the callous judge from your mind. That God doesn't exist. That's an unbiblical image people project onto Him. It's Christ's *love*, not His wrath, that sent Him to the cross. And it's Christ's *love*, not His wrath, that compels us to reach out to those who don't know Him yet.

Love is our motivation. Love is our method. Love is our strategy. Love is everything.

That's why when all else fails—when you think you don't know enough, aren't extroverted enough, or you're afraid you'll do something wrong—just love people into heaven.

Anybody can love.

KINDNESS IN ACTION

When Lisa and I moved to the suburbs of Philadelphia to start Christ's Church of the Valley, we didn't know a soul. There wasn't a core group of people waiting for us. There wasn't a supporting church to help us. If there was going to be a church, we were going to have to go out and find people.

Our strategy was simple. Our grand opening was set for the first Sunday in October of the year 2000, so we held three informational picnics over the summer. To get people there we passed out five thousand flyers before each one. Then as we connected with various individuals and families at the picnics, we invited them to a Bible study at our house on Sunday nights.

The picnics themselves were simple. About twenty minutes before people showed up, we cooked a pile of hot dogs and hamburgers, and then at six o'clock we started eating. After about thirty minutes of eating and mingling, Lisa would take the kids off to the side for a lesson and to play games, while I spoke about the vision for the church and asked people to join us.

Fifty-nine people came to the first picnic. Seventy-seven people came to the second picnic. The third picnic we held in our backyard. Fifty-five people showed up for that one. By and large, our strategy worked. By the end of the summer we had gathered exactly seventy people who signed up to join us. But it wasn't all smooth sailing.

I'll never forget our second picnic. You could feel the excitement in the air. Lisa took the kids over to the side and told them about God's love and played some fun, interactive games. Meanwhile I stayed back at the picnic tables and poured my heart out to the adults.

"This is going to be a different kind of church," I told them. "This is the kind of church anyone can come to."

For thirty minutes I simply shared my dreams for what this new community could do in the Philadelphia metro area and beyond.

Then I opened it up for questions.

A lady in the back quickly shot up her hand.

"Uh, the word on the street is that this is a cult."

People's faces immediately tensed up. The question took me by complete surprise, and because I wasn't quite sure how to respond, the awkwardness of the moment was palpable. Honestly, that was the very first time it had ever occurred to me that having the last name Jones, and starting a new church, was not a good thing.

The name Brian Jones reminded people of Jim Jones, that cult leader in Guyana who killed all those people—see the connection?

My first thought was to say, "Lady, I've got some special grape juice for you." But I didn't think that would come across real well.

I told her about our orthodox beliefs, my education, and the oversight we had in place to hold us accountable. That seemed to satisfy her and everyone else. That was the day I met Gene Marks. He had worked thirty years as a truck driver for a construction company in the area but had just retired. Relatives up near Bloomsburg, Pennsylvania, found out about our church through a mutual friend and had told Gene and his wife, Carol, about us, so they showed up to the picnic to see what this new church was all about. Gene walked up to me and said, "I'm in."

Abraham Heschel once said, "When I was young, I admired clever people. Now that I am old, I admire kind people."[3]

That pretty much described Gene's personality. Gene was a kind man. When the church started, Gene greeted people at the door. I'm not sure if anyone asked him to do it. He just started greeting people because that's what Gene did. He welcomed people.

I had the privilege of leading Gene to Christ and baptizing him just a few months after our church started, and from that point on he was a man on a mission. Rain, snow, or heat, it didn't matter; you could always find Gene standing at the doorway of the church, loving people and making them feel welcome. Gene was a quiet guy. Those who didn't know him would have never guessed that Gene had a bad heart, that he endured procedure after procedure just to keep it ticking.

When Gene wasn't greeting people at church, he was fishing with his buddies on the lakes and streams in our area. Gene loved people, loved Jesus, loved our church, and loved to fish. He owned a little boat that he put into the back of his pickup truck, and used that as a way to build friendships with his hard-core non-Christian buddies in the community. Every so often I'd see one of Gene's friends sneak into the back of church during a service. He was truly a fisher of men.

I'll never forget the day, six years after that first service, when we held the inaugural service in our own church building. The place was packed. Six long years of set up and tear down in a movie theater had come to an end. As we sang the first song to thank God for being so faithful to us over the years, I turned around and saw Gene and Carol sitting a few rows behind me.

Gene was bawling like a baby.

Gene loved lost people, and no one celebrated more joyously when someone found their way back to God than my retired, short, introverted, high school–educated, and soft-spoken friend Gene Marks. He welcomed them at the door, cried at their baptisms, took them fishing on his boat, and loved them into Christ's kingdom.

I know for a fact Gene didn't know a lot about the Bible.

He didn't have a lot of Scripture memorized.

I'll bet you anything he couldn't name two of the twelve apostles.

He didn't know the key differences between Christianity and other world religions.

He didn't have clever answers for unsuspecting atheists.

He didn't have a winsome, gregarious, "work the room" personality.

But Gene was a kind man, and he loved people, and that was enough. Over the last ten years of his life, which just so happened to be the first ten years of Christ's Church of the Valley, he had a direct hand in helping countless people connect to our church and come to faith in Christ.

I had the honor of conducting Gene's funeral this past year, and as in life, Gene was surrounded by all his fishing buddies. When the service was over, I greeted every single one of them on the way out. It was as if they had all gotten together beforehand and someone coached them on what to say. They all shared a funny fishing story. They all shared how Gene was a truly caring human being. And they all shared how much Gene helped them understand God and always asked them to come to church.

I don't know what your life has been like up to this point. I don't know what your personality is like, how long you've been following Christ, or whether or not you know a lot about the Bible. It really doesn't matter. All I know is that the legacy of this kind, unassuming man is going to echo through his friends' lives and on into eternity. And it all happened simply because he loved people.

You can do this.

I know you can.

Just love people into heaven.

NOTES

1. Rebecca Manley Pippert, *Out of the Saltshaker & Into the World* (Downers Grove, IL: InterVarsity Press, 1999), 113.

2. Richard Foster, *Prayer: Finding the Heart's True Home* (San Francisco: Harper-San Francisco, 1992), 1, quoted in Cheryl Bridges Jones, "Transformed by Grace: The Beauty of Personal Holiness," in *The Holiness Manifesto,* eds. Kevin W. Mannoia and Don Thorsen (Grand Rapids, MI: Eerdmans, 2008), 155.

3. Abraham Heschel, quoted in Jessica Gribetz, *Wise Words: Jewish Thoughts and Stories Through the Ages* (New York: HarperCollins, 1997), 36.

ADDITIONAL RESOURCES

Readers:

If you share the urgency of the message of this book, please take a moment and spread the word on Facebook, Twitter, Amazon.com, blogs, etc. I'd love nothing more than to see you be used by God to fire up your Christian friends to reach the non-Christians around them.

If you've been encouraged by the message of the book, I would love to hear from you! Please email me at brian@moviechurch.com.

Church Leaders:

For free *Hell Is Real (But I Hate to Admit It)* small-group study questions and church-wide sermon-series campaign materials—including free sermons, videos, images, and worship materials—please visit:

www.IfHellIsReal.com

More Information about Brian Jones:

To watch Brian's sermon videos online and find out more about other books he's written, please visit www.BrianJones.com.

ACKNOWLEDGMENTS

Much love and appreciation to …

Penny Whipps—for getting the ball rolling.

Jenni Burke—for sacrificially nurturing this book into existence.

Don Jacobson—for taking the risk.

My friends at David C Cook, for their partnership in the ministry of this book—especially (but not limited to) Alex Field, Renada Arens, Amy Konyndyk, Nick Lee, Karen Athen, Don Pape, Ginia Hairston Croker, Mike Salisbury, and Mike Ruman.

The entire CCV church staff—for taking the time to give me honest feedback as the chapters rolled off the printer.

Jeanne Lasko—for graciously taking the time to comb the manuscript for typos and inconsistencies.

Alyssa Dourte and Dan Reischel—for creating the small-group study guide.

Ben Foulke, David Wasserman, and Brett McFarland—for bringing the church-wide campaign to life (ideas, videos, images, etc.).

Kevin Stone—for his continuing friendship and support.

Kelsey, Chandler, and Cammy—for their understanding and support as their dad "buried himself in the cave" typing away.

Lisa—for graciously sharing the journey … in the words of the poet Mary Oliver,

I am so happy to be alive in this world
I would like to live forever, but I am
Content not to. Seeing what I have seen with you
Has filled me.